Reviews and Comments

When I started reading a prepublication copy of ***Animals I Have Hated***, I was transported back to when Herb Nordmeyer, a master storyteller, was being taught life lessons, as his mother illustrated points by telling about animals she had known. It renewed my appreciation of all of God's creatures, humans included.

C. C. from Texas

In his book ***Animals I Have Hated***, Herb Nordmeyer shares several chapters from his life's experiences to reinforce the values of compassion, forgiveness, kindness, understanding, and humor. I shared some of Herb's stories with my wife. She chuckled aloud at the humor and wanted to read the book for herself. It's a good book fit for young and old. I felt Herb's gentle wit combined with the special love he has for his mother to evoke emotions ranging from sadness on one end to laughter on the other end. I'll never forget about the cow Herb cleverly named *Magnesia*. He asks, "What better way to get *Milk of Magnesia*?" I still laugh to myself about that one. When Herb offers lessons from nurturing pets, raising farm animals, fishing, and being a student of nature, he reveals a profound appreciation for family and weathering life's storms. His stories and lessons serve as a reminder that none of us are without adversity and struggle. Life is better when you make light of life's problems through understanding and humor and count your blessings. After reading Herb's book, I was enriched with optimism, humbled through understanding, and appreciative of his generation's contributions.

Craig Jones, Cibolo, Texas

Patrick McManus meets country living. The stories are wonderful heart stories.

Deborah M. Salinas, Art/Technology Teacher

The title of this book is all wrong. Sure, this is no treehuggin', earth-kissin' book about how the author worshipfully enters some dreamtime trance and communes with his spirit animal, or the spirit of an animal that talks to him with words and flashy haloes like some New Age movie or a Disney production. You figured that out already.

But it's just really unfair to call this book *Animals I Have Hated,* when it's clear the author doesn't really hate most animals. In addition to liking them fried, roasted over a fire or hot plate, milked for cream and butter, and sold as stock for a little revenue, he lets them snooze under his couch (skunk), sleep draped around his neck (the ocelot-like margay), pose at the end of a camera lens (mosquito, cockroach), and sulk in a hastily-evacuated classroom (rattlesnake).

There's a lost world in this book, full of things that an ordinary city- or suburban-dweller will marvel at, like the knotholes in the floor boards where a vicious cat lurks, or a cistern that supplies both household water and also an unintentional yet irresistible lure for ducklings. Rattlesnake bites, hunting trips gone wrong, siblings whose pets have real murder in their hearts (the pets, not the siblings... well, mostly not the siblings). These are the howlarious stories that those "back to the land" romantics don't talk about while you're envisioning homesteading just like Laura Ingalls Wilder. Wake up! This is a Texas kind of homesteading—south Texas, that is. Cowboy up. I can almost feel the tablecloth stick to my sweaty forearms at the Nordmeyer family dinner table.

As an older sister, I cringe at the unexploited opportunities I missed to turn my siblings into the kind of revenue-generating sources so well-done in this book. The author is a very creative, very dedicated person, who has obviously set some goals for himself. Praiseworthy in this day and age. And mixed in with all the homespun wisdom about swimming in leech-filled ditches and pulling cactus spines from one's backside is real knowledge about real experiences working (really working) real jobs [that in this day and age would be grounds for OSHA intervention and potential lawsuits]. Amazingly, the author miraculously manages to live through all these experiences to show us that a writer can never truly have bad experiences because it can all be used as material.

Get a taste of real Texas living. Read this book! It explains so much about how we got this... colorful and jaunty. How tough folks had to be, just to live long enough to raise a family and get the last dinner roll. Hint: look out for that fork.

P.S. It is my sincere hope the author amends the title before the third printing run of this book. I think it will affect sales.

Jeanine Sih Christensen
http://www.greenbuilder.com
http://www.sustainablesources.com

While Herb Nordmeyer is a leading authority in the stucco industry, this book demonstrates that he excels when telling stories. When I picked up *Animals I Have Hated*, I could not put it down. Life lessons are slipped in so smoothly that they are part of the stories. He is endowed with dry wit that he uses in all of his writing, so even his treatises on stucco are fascinating reads. Somehow Herb finds time to be a wilderness kayaking guide. I'm looking forward to a book of stories about problems that occur when taking senior citizen neophytes into the wilderness

Joe Noonan, San Antonio, TX

Frontispiece

Momma and some of the animals I have known

Animals I Have Hated

Howl-arious Life Lessons Taught by Animals

Written by Herb Nordmeyer

Illustrated by Ciera Dela Cruz,
Breanne Ludovice, and Deborah M. Salinas

Nordmeyer, LLC
Castroville, TX
2012

ISBN   978-0-9847936-2-4

Library of Congress Control Number   2012902610

Illustrations by: Ciera Dela Cruz,
                                  Breanne Ludovice, and
                                  Deborah M. Salinas

Author portrait by: Joe Noonan

Cover design by: Janice Campbell
                                  The Very Idea
                                  San Antonio, TX
                                  www.theveryidea.biz

Library of Congress Subject Headings:
                                  Animal Behavior/Anecdotes
                                  Life Lessons
                                  Humorous Stories
                                  Country Life

Trademarks
        Sanforized is a registered trademark of The Sanforized Company.

Published by:
Nordmeyer, LLC
213 County Road 575
Castroville, Texas 78009-2120
www.NordyBooks.com

The Illustrators

Deborah Salinas has taught art and technology classes for 18 years. She enjoys working with children, seeking to provide them a creative venue in which to showcase their God-given talents. When she is not at work, she enjoys archery, crafts, reading, the beach, and playing with the family blue-heeler. She greatly enjoyed working with the young illustrators as they tackled the task of matching illustrations to Mr. Nordmeyer's words.

Ciera Dela Cruz is a junior high student with a complex about her height. She likes to stay home and watch British television shows and wishes more people would use umbrellas. While working on *Animals I Have Hated*, Ciera had to tweak her style, which happens to be Japanese comic art. She hopes that art will remain a possible career choice for her in the future.

Breanne Ludovice is a middle school girl who enjoys many things. Trying new things interests her as she learns more and more each day. In her free time, she reads, plays the piano or violin, illustrates, and makes crafts. Breanne's forte in drawing is Anime, which is known here as Japanese animated cartoons. She enjoys teaching others this style of art and creating drawings based on her friends' requests.

Dedication

To my wife Judy who has reviewed every draft of this book and of all of the other writing that I do. She takes my spelling errors and grammatical errors in stride and drips red ink over them. Even when Microsoft Word cannot figure out what I mean, she soldiers on. In payment, she gets to chuckle at my mistakes from time to time and listen to readers gush, "Isn't he wonderful."

To my mother, Louise Blankinship Nordmeyer, who was a pioneer and a master storyteller. When trying to convince her to write and publish the stories she told about animals, she said that if she did, she would call it *Animals I Have Hated*. Thus, I stole the title of this book from my own mother. How low will a storyteller stoop for a good title?

Table of Contents

Preface

This book is for you if you
Want to learn life lessons—they are slipped in,
Tell stories—because it is a wonderful source,
Want to learn about the "Good Old Days"—they weren't,
Want to laugh—it is hilarious,
Want to teach your children and grandchildren—and entertain them in the process,

Robert Fulghum wrote ***All I Really Need to Know I Learned in Kindergarten***. I never had the opportunity to go to kindergarten. In fact, I was nearly seven years old when I started first grade. As a result, I had to look elsewhere to learn what I needed to know to get along in life. Most of life's important lessons I learned from animals, either directly from them or from stories my mother told about animals she had encountered. This is a collection of those life lessons. Some are humorous. Some will make you cry. Some, such as the mama cat nursing a baby jackrabbit, will make you do both. All are included because they taught me something.

Over the years, one of the high points of family evenings together was when my mother would tell stories about the animals that were around our farm. Most of the stories illustrated a point that she wanted to teach us. My father also told stories to illustrate points, but his stories were not as related to animals as were my mother's stories.

With my upbringing, it was only natural that I should become a storyteller. Whether in a business meeting, at a church meeting, around a campfire, teaching a point to the younger relatives, or just having a conversation with friends, it was much easier to make a point by illustrating it with a story. Hopefully it would stress the point, so they would remember it longer. If not, at least I got to tell a story.

Over the years storytelling developed into a project I have worked on for the past fifteen years. I am one of the writers of the devotions that our church publishes. I start with a warm and fuzzy story and then relate it to a Biblical point. Several theologians have told me that this is the wrong way to do it. One should start with a Bible verse and expound on it. Usually I do not listen to them.

For years I encouraged my mother to write down the animal stories that she told. Each time she came up with a new reason why she should not write them down. One fall, I was short on money to buy Christmas presents, so I wrote some of the stories down and give her and my siblings copies. My father and I traded ties that neither of us would wear, so that would take care of all but one Christmas present. As I wrote, I inserted myself into many of the stories as an observer, even though I had not been born when the incident occurred. It seemed to make the stories more believable. I wrote the stories as I remembered them and included in the Foreword the following:

"At this time, I will guarantee that all of these stories are the truth as it was told to me, as I remembered it, or as I would like to have remembered it. In some cases, I have changed names to protect the guilty. If the guilty recognize my version of their deeds, then I am honored. If they don't, then they have faulty memories."

Christmas came, and each opened his/her slim little book(let). Soon I started getting flak. Each sibling accused me of picking on him. "You singled me out and made me look stupid," was a common comment. To this day, they remember how I picked on them in the book that I gave them. Not only did I pick on them, I did not get them a real Christmas present that year. After our mother's funeral, we talked about the book. All of them still had their copies, and they wanted me to make copies for those children and grandchildren who did not have copies. Why, after all of these years, have they kept their copies of the book if it was so bad? So I started writing.

The stories are arranged in some hybrid sequence that, on one dark and dreary night while listening for a raven to knock at my chamber door, made sense to me. Rather than come up with a new sequence, I'll let you decide whether the sequence makes sense.

Some will conclude that we mistreated animals. Maybe we did, but that was a different time. These stories relate what actually happened, or maybe I should say they relate the way I remember things happening. Many grandparents who grew up on small farms will be able to relate to the way we treated the animals we encountered.

Sit back, relax, enjoy, and learn a few of life's many lessons that I have learned.

Snake

Some days just do not go the way they are planned. Then when they are off going some different direction, they wander off in yet another direction. That happened when Jimmy was two years old.

"MommaMommathere'sasnakeunder-
mywheelbarrowcomeoutandkillit.
**MommaMommathere'sasnakeunder-
mywheelbarrowcomeoutandkillit.**"

Two-year-old Jimmy, my older brother, was talking as fast as his little mouth could move. His arms were thrashing back and forth as he nearly tore the screen door off its hinges and came running to Momma. Momma swept him up and tried to hug him still, but his arms and legs and mouth continued to work. Momma said, "Jimmy, slow down so I can understand you."

And after a time, he calmed down and hollered, "**MOMMA, MOMMA, THERE'S A SNAKE UNDER MY WHEELBARROW. COME OUT AND KILL IT.**" Momma saw an opportunity to be a hero in her son's eyes. She figured that you couldn't put much of a snake under a little wheelbarrow like that, so there wouldn't be much of a problem becoming a hero. As a result, she said, "Let's get a hoe, and we'll go kill your snake." They marched to the garage as if on a mission and got a hoe. Momma tested the edge and asked Jimmy if he thought it was sharp enough to kill a snake. "But Momma, it's a big snake." They walked around to the front yard where Jimmy's toy wheelbarrow lay upside down. The wheelbarrow's body was just over a foot long, eight inches wide, and about four inches deep. There just was not room for much of a snake under that wheelbarrow.

With Jimmy standing behind her skirts, she reached with the hoe and flipped the wheelbarrow over. Coiled beneath the wheelbarrow and filling all of the space under it was a black snake. Nowadays we call them indigo snakes, since they are midnight blue, but back then everyone called them black snakes. It lay there coiled up, looking at the intruders. No one moved, and then the snake's tongue came out. Again the tongue came out. After what seemed like an hour, the snake got tired of lying in the sun, and it slowly uncoiled and started to crawl off. As it crawled, Momma noted that it was several feet longer than she was tall, and she was five feet eight inches tall. Rather than vigorously attacking the snake with the hoe, she uttered a subdued "eek."

As the snake crawled under the house, Jimmy looked at it, and then he looked up at Momma to see if he could comprehend why she had let that snake crawl off. Apparently he did not find a satisfactory answer, but at two years of age he had sense enough to keep his mouth shut.

In later years, as the various ones of us were growing up, Jimmy taught us many things. But one of the prime things he taught us was that we had to kill our own snakes, 'cause Momma would not be any help. Even though we commonly referred to killing snakes, this is not something we literally did. We used it to refer to any problems we got ourselves into and were expected to get ourselves out of. Another common expression was, "I see you are digging your own grave." I do not remember any of us killing any real snakes, except for a few rattlesnakes that showed up in the yard.

Bantams For Breakfast

Recently I commented to my mother that I was going to get some bantams to use as setting hens. She warned me about not letting the bantams cross with the standard-sized chickens. I asked why not, so she told me this story.

"About fifty years ago, shortly after I married your father, we acquired several hens and some bantams. The bantam rooster, being an aggressive individual, soon had bantam and half-bantam progeny. As the chicks grew, they learned to fly and started roosting in the citrus trees behind the house. As each day passed, they grew a little wilder. Probably the only thing that kept them even half-tame was the hen scratch I fed them twice each day.

"Then, in the dark of night, sickness struck. First, I came down with a sore throat and fever. I was so sick I did not scratch the chickens. The next day I was worse. By the third day, the half-bantams had given up civilization and become wild fowl.

"After several days, your grandma decided that I needed nourishment and that chicken soup would provide such nourishment. She dispatched your father to the citrus orchard with a shotgun to bring back the makings for chicken soup. Shortly he returned with a half-bantam pullet about six weeks old. Soaking wet, it probably weighed twelve ounces. Your grandma made chicken soup, even utilizing the pencil-sized drumsticks. Rather than cut up the white meat, she left it whole for me to eat–two little pieces, each about two inches long. With the tray in front of me, I could not eat; I could only think of that poor, defenseless baby chick that your father and his mother-in-law had killed before it had an opportunity to enjoy life."

They fed me a poor, defenseless baby chick.

I asked Papa what became of the half-bantams. He said that after they grew to their adult size (two pounds), the family was going to move to a new home. Since it was impossible to capture the half-bantams, they were collected with a twenty-gauge shotgun. Besides being tough and undersized, they had lead shot in them.

I found it fascinating that each time Momma would tell the story, she referred to "your father and his mother-in-law." When your husband and your mother feed you chicken soup made from little chicks that are smaller than a quail, I guess one wants to establish as much distance as possible.

Animals I Have Hated

Kitty Nordmeyer

Grandma Nordmeyer hated cats. When she had kids around the house, whenever she had any say-so, they did not have any cats. So when Jimmy wanted a cat, Papa did not have enough experience with cats to be averse to letting Jimmy have a kitten. Jimmy ended up with a female kitten of the Heinz 57 variety, and promptly named the cat "Kitty," which he thought was a good name for a kitty. Grandma Nordmeyer would not let life be easy for two-and-a-half-year-old Jimmy. She informed him every chance she had that "Kitty" was not a good name for a cat. But Jimmy kept insisting that his kitty's name was "Kitty."

Grandma Nordmeyer had rubbed in the fact that "Kitty" was not a proper name for a kitty, until it wasn't fun anymore. She then asked Jimmy if "Kitty" had a last name. Jimmy insisted that his cat's name was "Kitty." One Sunday morning in church, when Momma, Papa, and Jimmy were sitting in the back row, Jimmy spotted Grandma Nordmeyer about six rows forward. He stood up; and in his best voice, which was known to drown out the preacher from time to time, announced, "Grandma, my kitty has a last name. My kitty's name is 'Kitty Nordmeyer'." If Grandma Nordmeyer could have sat any lower in her pew, she would have. After that announcement, the name "Kitty" was dropped, and "Kitty Nordmeyer" was henceforth known by her surname.

"Nordmeyer" grew up to be an excellent mouser. When there weren't enough mice in the house, under the house, in the barn, or in the sheds, she would head out into the open fields to catch mice. In due time, "Nordmeyer" became a mother. She took to motherhood like she took to mousing. She gave it her all. When her kittens were half-grown, she'd bring them mice. When they got into fights with other cats, she would do battle for them. There were times when she was feeding as many as three and four litters at the same time. None of her kittens turned out like "Nordmeyer." They were all good-for-nothing, free-loading cats. Momma watched the development of litter after litter. Since she did not have a great deal of education concerning the proper way to rear children, she learned by observation and concluded that if you gave your kid everything he wanted and always did battle for him, he would become a good-for-nothing free-loader. I can't remember Momma ever bringing home a mouse for us or beating up a cat, so I guess she learned her lessons well.

When Jimmy was about five years old, "Nordmeyer" had a kitten that was pure white and had baby blue eyes. When the kitten was about four months old, it fell into the outhouse pit.

Author's Note: *An outhouse was an outdoor toilet. It consisted of a little house, about three feet by four feet that sat over a pit that had been dug in the ground. A board was placed at a convenient height and had one or two holes cut in it, so it could serve one or two people at a time. Very modern ones occasionally had a toilet seat attached over the holes, but we were never modern. When the smell got bad, a little lime was thrown down the hole. When the hole was nearly full, another pit was dug, the outhouse was moved, and the old pit was covered with dirt. We were careful to not walk across those areas for a number of months because one could sink into the pit.*

A few days later, Cousin Al came to visit Jimmy, so Jimmy told him about the white cat which turned brown. While Momma and Al's mother went shopping and Grandma babysat, a plan was hatched.

Jimmy caught "Nordmeyer," and Al got a broom. They then headed to the outhouse, opened the lid, and with the broom pushed "Nordmeyer" under. An hour later, when the mothers got home from shopping, they found Grandma holding "Nordmeyer"

Animals I Have Hated

under a water faucet scrubbing her. Grandma was muttering about modern kids with no discipline and a cat named "Nordmeyer." As much trouble as she was going to, I wondered whether she hated "Nordmeyer" as much as she hated all cats.

Many years later we found that many white cats with blue eyes were deaf. My sister, Nancy, had one that would follow us out to the mailbox, about seventy-five feet from the door of our home, and if we abandoned the cat out there, it would get lost and not know how to find its way home. It would sit there and meow until someone came and found it. Nancy would be furious every time we did it, whether we did it on purpose or inadvertently.

When "Nordmeyer" was about eight years old, she had still another batch of kittens. When they were about three days old, Papa found a two- or three-day-old creature in one of the irrigation canals. It was without fur and had short ears and a short tail. After eliminating coons, possums, dogs, cats, skunks, weasels, rats, and mice, he decided to take it home and add it to "Nordmeyer's" litter. The creature was accepted by "Nordmeyer" and by its litter mates. Within a few days, fur developed; and about the time its eyes opened, its ears began to elongate. Soon we recognized the creature for what it was–a young jackrabbit.

When the jackrabbit was about three weeks old, we discussed around the supper table one evening how a rabbit would fit in with our menagerie of cats and dogs. We came to no conclusions; however, the problem solved itself. The next morning we found "Nordmeyer" and her kittens dining on the young jackrabbit.

Momma would usually tell only part of the story, and the part was selected to illustrate a point. If I was teasing my little sisters, she might tell about the naming of "Kitty Nordmeyer" to illustrate that the younger generation should not be pushed into a corner. If I wanted to bring another animal home, then I might hear about the young jackrabbit that was so much a part of "Nordmeyer's" family until she recognized that it had a new purpose in her life. I would

Kitty Nordmeyer

be asked how the new animal would fit into our lives. If I commented that I could not stand someone, I would hear about Grandma washing the cat that she stated that she detested and be asked if Grandma really hated that cat or if it was just a show. Momma really did use "Nordmeyer" not only to teach her correct child rearing, but she used her to teach her children. Many a time, when I would ask permission to do something, she would ask how "Nordmeyer" would handle it. I would think about it and respond, usually giving me permission to do what I wanted to do. She would then ask how "Nordmeyer's" children had turned out. It was difficult to fight that logic.

Something Awful

Even though "Nordmeyer" had been keeping us in kittens, we were regularly given kittens by Aunt Benny and Uncle Zara. Aunt Benny was not much over five feet tall. Uncle Zara was well over six feet tall. Both were slender. Uncle Zara was the only person I have ever known who could declare with a straight face that any kitten we were interested in was a boy. One morning, more years ago than I can count, we visited Aunt Benny and Uncle Zara. As we sat on the screened porch, Uncle Zara looked at me and said, "Would you like to see our kittens?" The answer to that was self-evident, and shortly my brothers Jimmy and Bill were crowding me out of the way so they could look at the kittens that were nursing. Uncle Zara said, "If you ask your mother, she will let you take one home." Jimmy responded, "Only if it is a male." Bill said, "That one is mine."

After thirty minutes of tense negotiation, Jimmy, Bill, and I were each allowed to select a kitten. Bill selected a gray kitten. I selected another gray kitten. Jimmy selected a yellow kitten. Uncle Zara looked at each and declared that each was a male. Even as a first grader, I knew about Uncle Zara and sexing kittens. He would pick up any kitten that we wanted and declare that it was a male. He was right about twenty percent of the time. In later years I learned that others who got kittens from Uncle Zara did their own sexing and took males, so by the time we selected kittens, there were more females than males. This did not bother us, but Momma insisted that we have only male cats.

For once, Uncle Zara was accurate. Both Bill's and my kittens were tomkittens. Jimmy–well, we will not discuss that aspect. Over the next week, we argued about the naming of our kittens and over which kitten belonged to which kid. Finally, Papa had enough of the arguing. He stated that he was going to name the kittens after each of us. The yellow kitten he named Bad, and stated that it belonged to Jimmy. The long-haired gray kitten he named Awful, and stated that it belonged to me. The other gray kitten he named Worse, and stated that it belonged to Bill.

Bill and I did not mind the names, since we got the kittens we had originally chosen. Jimmy did not mind the name of his kitten, since it showed that he was better than his brothers.

As with all kittens, these kittens grew and soon were half-grown alley cats. Along about this time Bad disappeared. Awful was devoted to me and followed me everywhere. Worse grew also, but he never bonded to Bill the way Awful bonded to me.

I decided that Awful needed to learn tricks. Bill told me that you taught tricks to dogs, not cats. Jimmy laughed at me. I continued, and before long Awful started learning tricks. Our favorite one involved me throwing him on the roof, and then he would jump down on my shoulders. As long as I did not flinch, he did not dig his claws in. As months passed, the rest of the family would always look up at the roof before walking into the house or the tractor shed. They did not like Awful landing on their shoulders, but they knew enough not to flinch.

As time went by, Awful grew to what we considered his full weight. He was a very muscular tomcat with very long, very thick, blue-gray fur. I insisted that it was two inches long, but Jimmy finally got out a ruler and determined that it was only one-and-seven-eighths-inches long. He told me that he did not want to hear any more about my cat with two-inch-long fur. He said that since he had measured it, to say it was two inches long was a lie.

Since then I have heard of cats that looked like Awful, but were much lighter in weight and had shorter fur, called Russian Blues.

Animals I Have Hated

When he was about eight months old, we decided to weigh him on a cotton scale. Decided is the key word, since he did not agree. First we weighed an empty sack. Then we stuffed Awful into the sack and tied the top. As the sack jumped around and screeched like a banshee, we grabbed it and hung it from a cotton scale. After re-hanging the bouncing and screeching sack on the scale several times and dodging a leg with five sharp claws that worked a hole in the sack, we determined that Awful weighed eight pounds. We set the sack on the ground, and I opened the top. Awful departed. Momma took the cotton sack into the house to make repairs.

Awful was not present for breakfast the next morning. I knew that we had offended him to the extent that he would never come back. Then, the following morning as I dejectedly walked to the shed to get Pet milk, Awful landed on my shoulders and knocked me down. I was forgiven. Even though Awful lived many years and put on more weight, we never weighed Awful again. I cannot remember us even discussing weighing him again.

After Awful reached one year of age, he was even more muscular, and he became the dominant tom in our area. Other tomcats disappeared, including Worse. After he had established his territory around our small farm, he started extending his territory. We received reports that he was seen a quarter of a mile south at the Garza house and a quarter of a mile north at Uncle Carlos' house. Uncle Carlos complained that Awful was knocking their cats off the roof of their two-story house. What could we do? Cats own people; people don't own cats.

Months passed, and Awful would meet me every morning as I headed out to milk our cow named Pet. When I got Pet milk for the family, he wanted his share. Awful could catch a stream of milk better than any of the other cats. Maybe he had more practice since I was more inclined to respond to his requests. Many times Awful came in bloody and with ragged ears, looking like he had been in an awful fight. By definition, any fight that he was in was an Awful

Fight. No matter how much tomcatting he did, he was always there for breakfast as I milked Pet.

One day Momma went over to see Aunt Lee. The second son of their family, Rob, was reading a book about Africa. The title was "Lion." Aunt Lee sent Rob on an errand; but since Rob was engrossed in the book because he was at a part where a male lion was stalking a white hunter, he ignored the request. Aunt Lee reiterated the request in stronger terms. Rob continued to read as he walked from the kitchen to the back porch and out onto the patio. As the lion sprang at the white hunter, Awful dropped off the porch roof and landed on Rob's shoulders.

Rob felt the weight of the lion hit his shoulders. He tried to dodge, but the lion sunk his twenty claws into his shoulders and latched onto his scalp with jaws that could crush bones in an instant. Rob dropped the book; and as he tried to fight off the lion, he fell to the ground screaming. The lion might have killed him and eaten him then and there, but Momma and Aunt Lee heard the screams and rushed to the patio. On her way through the kitchen, Momma grabbed a broom. Brooms were her favorite weapons during any crisis. Upon reaching the patio, Momma assessed the situation. Awful had Rob down on the patio and was holding on. Rather than swat him with the broom, she commanded, "Awful! That is enough." Awful looked at her, for he knew her expertise with a broom, let go of Rob, and headed south towards the orange grove. Rob looked up in time to see the north end of a southbound Awful disappear into the trees. In time Rob recovered from his wounds, but the attack by the lion would remain clear in his memory for the rest of his life.

Momma came home and related the story. Rob was older than me, so I could not tease him or do anything that would give him justification to beat me up. Whenever he was around, I took to throwing Awful up onto the roof and letting Awful jump to my shoulders. I did not say anything, and neither did Rob, but he suspected that I was laughing at him for being such a sissy. If this

Animals I Have Hated

had kept up for long, I would have developed sufficient muscles so I could have gone out for shot put. Two weeks after the lion attacked Rob, Awful did not show up for breakfast. This was the first time he had skipped breakfast since we weighed him. I was heartbroken. I tried throwing other cats on the roof, but they just ran when they landed on the roof. After a time or two, they ran when I looked at them.

The following morning, Awful was not at breakfast. That was two days in a row. He was not there the third day, or the fourth day. Each day was longer than the one before, and Awful still did not come. We heard that Rob had shot a cat that was in their orchard, and I wondered if Rob had shot Awful. When I asked him, he walked away.

We didn't see Awful for ten days. Then as I entered the shed to get the feed for Pet to eat while I milked her, I heard a low meow. Awful was lying on the floor of the shed. On his left shoulder was a large gaping hole. It was infected. I could see pus. He was skin and bones, and his hair was severely matted. I petted him briefly on the top of his head. His head was hot. He had a fever. He had come home to die. I realized that his love for me was the only thing that had brought him home. I told Awful to be strong and wait for me, and then I did the only thing that a third grader could do in a crisis. I headed to the house to get Momma. She came out and examined Awful's wound while I carefully petted Awful's head. She said that there was nothing we could do for the wound. He would lick it and hopefully get it cleaned. Jimmy milked Pet that morning and brought me a small bowl of milk. I held the bowl in one hand and Awful's head in the other hand. He lapped a few laps of milk but was too exhausted to continue. After one more feeding before the school bus came, Momma told me that if I missed the school bus, she would take her broom to me. With a heavy heart, I caught the school bus.

I could not concentrate on schoolwork, and after what seemed like fifteen years I caught the school bus home. During the day

Something Awful

Jimmy had told Rob about Awful being shot. Rob got off at our house and stopped in to see how Awful was doing. When he saw the gaping wound, he looked like he was going to get sick and wanted to know who would do a thing like that.

Awful was lying where he had been that morning. Momma had some milk warmed up for him, and I held his head and the bowl while he lapped a little milk. Except when I had to do chores or go in and eat, I spent the evening with Awful and about every two hours fed him some milk. His condition did not seem to change.

The next morning, Awful was in the same location, and I fed him again. He lapped a little more milk than before. When I told Momma that I had to stay home and feed Awful, she wanted to know if her feeding him the day before was inadequate. As she reached for the broom, I headed out for the school bus.

Rob came home with us again and was very concerned about Awful and who had shot him. Awful appeared a little better.

Day three—Awful would lick his wound after he had eaten. Rob came home with us again.

Day four—Awful was up on the feed box when I went out in the morning. Rob came home with us again. That evening we discussed the type of bullet that had been used on Awful. Due to the extent of the wound, we decided that it was a twenty-two long rifle hollow point. Rob said that they only used their twenty-twos for target practice and only had twenty-two shorts.

Author's Note: *Every farm family had at least one twenty-two-caliber rifle. They were referred to as twenty-twos. Many boys, as young as eight years of age, used them without supervision. A twenty-two shoots bullets that are twenty-two-hundredths of an inch in diameter. The boxes of ammunition warned that the projectiles could travel a mile. The ammunition came in several grades. "Shorts" have the least amount of gun powder, so they were the least powerful and cheapest. "Longs" were more powerful. The "long rifles" were the most powerful. Then there were* *the "long rifle hollow points." These had a hole in the end of the lead projectile and would explode on impact.*

Awful's recovery took about a month. He started taking an interest in his appearance after about two weeks. I helped by clipping out grass burrs and tangles. I thought about getting Nancy's (my sister) hairbrush and brushing Awful, but I was afraid that I might break the wound open. After the wound healed, he was stiff for an extended period of time. He took to riding around on my neck, like a fur stole. I did not throw him up on a roof because I was afraid that I would hurt him. After about three months, as I was going out to milk Pet, he dropped onto my shoulders. Awful was well.

During the next few months, Awful proceeded to clean the tomcats out of his territory and was known to go to Uncle Carlos' house and knock their cats off the second-story roof. This was a scientific experiment on Awful's part to see if cats always landed on their feet. Rob got mad at Awful, but I pointed out to Rob that **he** had thrown cats off the second-story roof to see if they would land on their feet. He said that was different. I was not old enough to understand teenagers.

About a year after the shooting, Awful moved to town and terrorized northwest Edinburg. Every month or so he would come back for a visit, but it was plain that he had found better tomcatting there and intended to stay. He lived for several years after that, and most kittens born in the area had long gray fur.

I guess we will never know who shot my Awful cat. If I knew, I would have to decide whether to hate that person or to forgive him for what he did nearly sixty years ago. Momma always told me that hating only hurt the hater. Over time I learned that sometimes it is just better to not know all of the facts.

Ducks Unlimited

After my grandfather died in 1940, Papa's heart was not in the family engineering business, officed in McAllen, Texas, so within a few months, he sold his share of the business to his brother-in-law. Since he had always wanted to farm, he arranged to farm with a farmer in Edinburg, my Uncle Carlos. My parents and their two oldest sons moved into the upstairs of his two-story farm house. As soon as he could, Papa constructed a one-room home for us using fifty dollars worth of used lumber, and the family moved in. The home was fourteen feet wide and twenty feet long. Shortly thereafter, he added a water system.

Author's Note: *The water system consisted of a line from an irrigation canal (where we swam), a slow sand filter, a thousand-gallon cistern, and a pitcher pump. While this system may sound crude, to us it was luxury. We didn't have to haul our water in fifty-five-gallon drums anymore. When we filled the cistern, we sanitized the water by pouring a quart bottle of Clorox into the cistern and stirring the water with a shovel. The only thing the system lacked was a lid on the cistern. Until we added indoor plumbing after WWII, we had to fill the cistern only about once per month. After we got indoor plumbing, when we had seven people living in that house, our water usage got up to nearly twenty gallons per person per day, and we had to fill the cistern once a week.*

After assessing our resources and needs, one of my well-meaning but very misguided aunts (who shall remain nameless) gave us a dozen duck eggs and loaned us a setting hen.

We placed the hen and duck eggs, along with our other chickens, in a henhouse Papa had built to protect them from varmints. During the day, the door was opened, and the hens could forage and drink from a pan we provided. At night the door was closed and barred. During that peaceful time while the hen incubated the eggs, we thought about the roast duck we would be eating within a few months. Then what we later came to view as a disaster struck. All twelve eggs hatched. The hen had a little problem adjusting to the fact that she had hatched some malformed (especially the beaks and feet) chicks; but after two days, she settled down to raising them.

The first duckling fell into the cistern when it was about a week old. After swimming around in our drinking water for a time and letting nature take its course, it started to sink, since it had no oil on its feathers. Just before it drowned, we caught it in a bucket swung from a hoe.

We should have wrung that duckling's neck, for later that day he returned to the cistern and took several friends with him. Over the next several weeks, we were constantly trying to cover the cistern with boards in a manner that would keep the ducklings out, while the ducklings were looking for holes. As the ducks matured, laid eggs, and hatched them, they would lead their ducklings to the cistern, even though the adults could not slip through the cover. After several years, the problem was solved when we poured a concrete cover for the cistern. We had a sheet metal lid made for the concrete cover. Protecting our water from ducks cost more than our house had cost.

We could have lived with the water problem. But the flock, which quickly grew to thirty or more, soon learned that food was delivered to them by people who exited the house by the back door. To be closer to the food supply, they moved from the chicken house to the back steps. By this time, we had a pen attached to the chicken house to keep the ducks away from our home. One of my jobs was to go out and cut Johnson grass for them several times per

Ducks Unlimited

day. We would herd the ducks back to the pen and chicken house, but even when we clipped one wing on each of them, they learned to fly over the chicken yard fence. The back doorstep got slick, and the flies multiplied. In polite language, it was one stinking mess.

We could have lived with the water problem.

We ate duck as often as we caught one, usually once or twice per week. Still they multiplied.

Cleaning a duck is time-consuming, since they have numerous pinfeathers and down. When the operator of the local locker plant offered to butcher the ducks at thirty-five cents each, over a period of two days we ran all the ducks down and carted them to town.

Author's Note: *After the concept of freezing food to preserve it developed, but before home freezers became common, there were businesses where you could rent a locker to store frozen food. These facilities were known as locker plants. Often these facilities were associated with facilities that butchered animals. The last locker plant I remember hearing about was in Austin, Texas, in the early 1970s.*

Animals I Have Hated

How could that man make money picking pinfeathers and down at that price? When we started to prepare the first duck, we found out. He didn't remove either the pinfeathers or the down. I guess the ducks won again, and we got "down in the mouth." Over the years when I thought I had found a really good deal, Momma would remind me of the man at the locker plant who butchered the ducks for us. It was only in later years that I realized why the French developed so many duck sauces. They were used to hide the pinfeathers and the down.

Recently, I seriously offended my brother-in-law. He took the worst possible revenge on my wife and me that he could. He gave us a bantam hen with three ducklings.

Carlos

Uncle Carlos lived down the road a quarter of a mile. He was Papa's older sister's husband, so to a certain extent he thought it was his duty to take care of his younger relatives, whether they thought they needed taking care of or not. When Momma was in her early thirties, I gave her chickenpox. While she broke out all over, the spots that bothered her most were on her face. Each day, Uncle Carlos would come past to help out. He could've helped out by changing Nancy's diaper. He could've helped out by washing dishes. He could've helped out by pumping water from the cistern. He could've helped out by emptying the slop bucket. But no, Uncle Carlos thought he was answering to a higher calling by holding a mirror where my mother could see all of the chickenpox on her face. Is it any wonder that on more than one occasion she referred to him as "my son's father's sister's husband?" Perhaps she didn't appreciate being related to him? I never heard her say a bad word in describing Uncle Carlos, but we all learned how to distance ourselves from someone emotionally.

Skunked

The Wares (cousins) and our family were visiting Uncle Carlos' family one Sunday afternoon when Uncle Carlos' oldest son, Carlito, observed a skunk entering a culvert under the road. Carlito passed the word, and soon Uncle Carlos decided to do away with the skunk before it caused problems or got inside the chicken coop. While I climbed to the top of a large mesquite tree to watch, Uncle Carlos built a fire on the upwind end of the culvert and posted Jimmy by the fire to keep it smoking. Johnny Ware and Rob, Uncle Carlos' second son, retreated to the haymow. Carlito and Uncle Carlos hid near the downwind end of the culvert to kill the skunk when it was smoked out.

The calm before the storm

Rather than follow the plans made for it, the skunk headed upwind and soon came face-to-face with Jimmy. Jimmy attacked. The skunk attacked.

I never found out what became of the skunk, but we did learn that none of the de-skunking remedies work. After an hour, the odor didn't bother Jimmy. I could smell him for several weeks.

Before Jimmy was ready for polite company, I overheard Johnny's mother telling how Johnny had killed a skunk and how one of his cousins, who ran from the skunk, got sprayed. I told Jimmy about how brave Johnny had been with the second skunk. Jimmy snorted and said, "Same skunk." I asked him which cousin got sprayed, but he just walked off. I guess he must have been mad at Johnny for killing the skunk that got away from him. I never did find out which cousin ran and got sprayed during the second skunk war.

When I got a little older, it dawned on me that there was only one skunk, and it got away; therefore, Johnny did not kill a skunk. I asked Momma about the story Johnny Ware's mother told. She said that when people do not perform up to their own expectations, they often stretch the truth to make them look better in their own eyes and in the eyes of friends. She never even hinted that my aunt was lying. She never explained to my satisfaction how a person can tell a lie that they know is a lie and then believe that lie. When I asked her about it, she said, "That is the way some people are made." I learned that I should not condemn people just because they are weak and embroider things to make themselves look better in their own eyes. I also learned that you cannot believe everything you are told.

Archie

Archie was Jimmy's dog, but he adopted all of us. While we questioned his breeding, for he was about the ugliest dog I have ever seen, there was no question as to his loyalty. We were his people, and he intended to defend us.

One of Archie's habits was to chase cars; however, chasing bicycles was his forte. He would end up with his jaws, dripping saliva, inches from the right ankle, never the left ankle, of the biker, all the while barking as if he was trying to blow the bike over. Experienced bikers (that is, experienced with Archie) ignored him and pedaled on. Two hundred yards down the road, Archie would determine that he had chased the threat to the family away and return home and lie down under the edge of the house where he could not be seen by an approaching bicyclist.

Archie protected us from serious threats.

Inexperienced bikers were a different matter. I learned first aid practicing on them. For some reason, the inexperienced biker would get nervous with Archie's one-and-a-half-inch fangs so close to his right ankle and would kick at Archie. Archie tolerated a lot, but he objected to people kicking at him. At the first and only kick, Archie would grab the biker's calf. With the fangs sunk to full depth, he would stop. Invariably, the biker would fall off his bike and start bleeding like a stuck pig, at which point Archie would let go and become very docile, but the biker would continue to cower in fear of that vicious dog. Thus, I became experienced in applying first aid to dog bites on the right calf of male bikers. I wonder if I could have treated a left calf.

Author's Note: *In this day and time, Archie would be considered a vicious dog, and the authorities would have put him down; but this was the 1940s, and things were different. Archie was protecting his family. After recovering, more than one of Archie's victims would get off their bikes and walk them past the house, talking to Archie as they walked. Archie would quietly escort them past the house and then return to his station.*

One spring Archie got sick. At first, we joked that he had bitten the wrong person. As he got worse, the joking stopped. Soon, he was just a mangy hide covering a skeleton, and we waited for him to die.

Author's Note: *Veterinarians were for economic animals—cows, pigs, and goats—not pets. Even though Archie protected us, we considered him a pet.*

One morning he dragged himself a few feet as we were going to catch the school bus; and as I petted him goodbye, I knew I would have to dig a grave when I got home. I decided that I would skip school, but Momma told me that she would get her broom, so with a heavy heart I got on the school bus.

Momma had watched Archie's suffering and decided to put him out of his misery. Rather than shoot him, she induced him to eat rat poison. Not a lethal dose, but ten times a lethal dose, so he would go quickly. He didn't. He started vomiting. For an hour he vomited. He then laid down and slept until the school bus brought us home. Even though he could barely stand, he met us at the bus. His appetite came back, and he recovered. Archie lived to chase bikes for several more years. We learned that sometimes it takes very desperate measures to cure a problem, and we should not just focus on the obvious solution.

Rabbit

Author's Note: *The land around Edinburg is alluvial over a layer of clay. This did not create a problem until the land was irrigated in order to grow crops. With each passing year the perched water table would rise a few inches, and soon it was close enough to the surface so capillary action would carry water to the surface. As the water evaporated, salts were left on the surface of the land. These salts had a negative impact on crop production. As a result, drainage ditches were installed, and drain lines were installed across fields.*

I found a wonderful private bathroom.

Watching a machine dig a trench that was five feet deep and about fifteen inches wide was a wonderful occupation for a five-year-old boy. Usually the equipment operator would have me stand so he could see me. Occasionally we would talk. On one of the occasions while watching the trenching operation, the equipment operator caught a young cottontail rabbit. He gave it to me, and I took it home. While the rabbit grew fast, he learned that boys and girls should be avoided. After we had had him for two weeks, the only time he would come out would be after we kids had gone to bed. He would then visit with Momma and Papa. The rabbit had only one bad habit. He selected an area under the head of my parents' bed as his bathroom. Since cardboard boxes were stored under the bed, it was difficult to clean up after him. As a result, I had to take the rabbit out and turn it loose.

This was not the only rabbit we had dealings with. Besides cottontails, we also had jackrabbits. Often while traveling along the turn rows of fields while headed for some brush country to explore, I would find a jackrabbit tied at the end of a row while one of the hands was using the tractor in the field. When I asked Papa why they caught tough jackrabbits rather than tasty cottontails, he demonstrated the technique while giving an explanation. Jackrabbits are smart, and cottontails are stupid. When you scare up a cottontail with a tractor, it takes off running. When you scare it up again, it makes another mad flight. A jackrabbit learns. The first time it hops away. The second time it hops a shorter distance. By the third or fourth time, it takes a few steps to get out of the tractor's path and watches the tractor as it passes. As we watched a jackrabbit step out of the way, Papa got off the tractor with it still in gear and still running. The furrows kept it headed where it needed to head. With the jackrabbit watching the tractor, he stepped behind the rabbit and grabbed it by its ears. Holding the rabbit, he remounted the tractor and took it out of gear. After examining the rabbit and petting it a little bit, we turned it loose. Papa then explained that if he had killed it, and not headed back to camp almost immediately, the meat would spoil. This is why the hands tied the rabbits at the ends of the row. If it was near quitting time, they would normally hit the rabbit with a wrench. A dead rabbit does not bite and scratch as much as a live rabbit.

When I wanted to catch a few jackrabbits, Papa told me that it was too dangerous for me to get off and then get back on a moving tractor, especially carrying a live jackrabbit. The tractor drivers did it all the time, and he did not tell them that it was too dangerous. I learned that there were higher standards that I was expected to meet. Logic did not change the fact that I was expected to meet a higher standard.

Cattle I Have Known

In 1938, when my brother Bill was three months old, he started crying. Any time he wasn't eating, he was crying. After Grandma was consulted and couldn't find the answer, Momma took Bill to the doctor. For a fee of five hard-earned dollars, the doctor told Momma that Bill was hungry. He advised her that she should buy a cow.

A local dairy was culling its herd, so Papa went and looked them over. The dairyman pointed out one small Jersey cow, which he said was not aggressive enough to make a good herd cow, but would make a good family cow. Papa bought the cow, and Momma named her Petunia. Bill had plenty of milk and quit crying. As the family grew, Petunia's milk production grew. Petunia had a calf that was named Rosebud; she became a family pet.

My mother, as did many other women in the Lower Rio Grande Valley of Texas at that time, started avocado trees from seed and hoped to raise avocados. Some did well; others died (the avocado plants, not the women). She had one plant that was doing extremely well. It had reached a height of four feet and was very bushy. Neighbors from three blocks away would come to admire it.

When my parents moved to Edinburg, they packed all of their possessions, including their kids, in the Model T, set the avocado plant on the bumper, tying it in place (even though four of the neighbors wanted it), tied Rosebud to the bumper, and set off for Edinburg. Rosebud got hungry. By the time the family reached Edinburg, the avocado plant was a stub. It never came out. The finger marks on Rosebud's throat (from Momma's choking her) faded with time. Momma would tell us this story when we were trying her patience, and she wanted to deliver the message that she could lose her temper if pushed too far.

Rosie loved Momma's beautiful avocado tree.

Author's note: *I never remember Momma losing her temper, yelling at anyone, or cursing, but she had a way with words. I remember her calmly informing a door-to-door salesman, "I hope your mother does not come out from under the porch and bite you." From the expression on his face and the way he beat a hasty retreat, I could tell he got the message.*

Once we had moved to the farm, all of Petunia's calves were sired by a bull named Prince. Not necessarily the same bull, but the same name. Uncle Carlos owned the adjoining farm and considered himself a well-to-do farmer. Since all well-to-do farmers with cattle tried to improve their herds, it was only natural that he would try to improve his herd. To do this, he owned a series of milking shorthorn bulls, each of which he named Prince.

When he wanted to keep the bull away from the cows, and he did not have enough separate pasture space, Uncle Carlos would stake his bull out in areas of good grazing. One Prince liked to travel at a full gallop. Regularly he would drag Uncle Carlos across a field. Uncle Carlos never let go of the chain. Whenever Prince dragged him, he would holler, "Damned old Bitch. Damned old Bitch. Damned old Bitch." We could hear him half a mile away. To us youngsters it was confusing; as Jimmy once said, "He's a bull, not a mama dog."

One day the hollering stopped, even though Prince continued to drag Uncle Carlos. Momma asked Lynda, his wife. She said, "The other day, one of the cats scratched Rob, our number two son. He threw it down and hollered those words. Uncle Carlos wanted to know where Rob had picked them up, so I told him." Momma would tell us this story when she thought we needed some motivation. If Uncle Carlos could abruptly cut off using what we considered were his favorite words, then we could set out to do anything we decided to do.

Regularly, Prince would get loose to visit our cows. Once he got into our garden. Momma took after him with a hoe. Rather than stand his ground, that sixteen-hundred-pound bull ran from that one-hundred-and-sixteen-pound woman and cleared the four-foot fence around the garden with ease. While Momma never bragged about her ability to chase larger animals, we learned that a strong attack against a much bigger enemy often carried the day. We never dared ask her why she said "eek" when the big black snake crawled away from Jimmy's toy wheelbarrow. It was nowhere near as big as that bull.

In due time, Petunia had a heifer calf which we named Pet. We kept her as a milk cow, since Petunia was growing old. Where Petunia was a calm, non-aggressive cow, Pet had a mind of her own. Regularly, she jumped the fences or crawled under them. One year I received a pair of fencing pliers for Christmas. It made my job of mending fences easier, but she still got out. On that November day in 1944 when Harry Truman was elected to the highest office in the land, Pet had a calf. Papa, being a good and loyal

Democrat, named the calf Harry. Harry had personality; when he was a day old, he started kicking people as he walked past them. By the time he was three days old, he would wait until you thought he was clear past, and then kick. Momma sometimes told us that most politicians were like Harry–they would kick you when you were not expecting it.

Author's Note: *We did not have garbage pickup and did not have a garbage can on the farm. We dug a pit about five feet wide by eight feet long and about five feet deep in the pasture. We would place our garbage in the pit and burn it. When the pit would be about eighteen inches from full, we would cover it up and dig another pit.*

When we took garbage out to the pit, Harry would follow us and then try to keep us in it. More than once we had to ask ourselves whether we would prefer to stay in the fire or face a playful young bull. I just could not understand why Momma could chase a sixteen-hundred-pound bull, but I could not intimidate a five-hundred-pound bull calf. In time I learned about pecking order and that Harry considered that I was beneath him in the pecking order. Revenge was sweet. I sure enjoyed eating Harry after we butchered him.

Cattle drink a lot of water. One of Bill's jobs was to fill the water tank every day. The cattle would come when they saw Bill start to work, and it seemed that they could empty the tank faster than he could fill it. He found that he could drive them from the tank and get it full; however, by the time our father came in, it would be empty, and Bill would have to explain how it could be empty if he had filled it an hour before. I can't remember a single time his answer was considered satisfactory.

In due time, Pet had another heifer calf. I named her Magnesia, for we intended to keep her as a milk cow, and we would be able to drink Milk of Magnesia.

As long as the cow is giving milk, she needs to be milked twice a day and milked until all of the milk has been taken. While the process seems simple, it takes a while to develop the muscles in the forearms in order to milk effectively. During the process, the cow will often swing her tail and hit the milker. Cartoons used to show a milker tying a brick to a cow's tail to keep from getting hit. We never tried that, but I can assure you that a cow could swing a couple of brick at the end of her tail and make a lethal weapon out of them. Additionally, the cow sometimes would move her foot and step on the milker's foot. That hurt, and sometimes she was slow to remove it. At other times, and this was especially true of Pet, the cow would kick. I always kept my forearm at the crook of Pet's kicking leg so I could control any kick aimed at me. Having a milk cow teaches discipline. There was never an acceptable excuse for being late for a milking, and Momma always woke me up before 6:00 am so I could get out for the morning milking. Evening milking was before we sat down to supper. Usually when we milked, the cats would join us and beg for a stream of milk.

After I finished milking the cow, we strained the milk through a dish towel, and then refrigerated the milk so the cream would rise. We did not know what homogenization (treating so the cream does not separate) and pasteurization (heat-treating to kill some of the bacteria in the milk) were. After the cream had risen to the top, it would be skimmed off, and we would use it to make butter. Real butter, not the butter that could be purchased in stores or the fake butter that comes in tubs. Cream is turned into butter by stirring or shaking. We had a device that was not unlike an ice cream freezer with a crank on it. After turning the handle for a time, we would open it up, strain out the chunks of butter, and place them in a wooden mold. After filling the wooden mold, we would remove the one-pound chunk of butter and refrigerate it. If we had too much butter, the local HEB was always glad to take it off our hands in trade for other groceries. Oleomargarine came out in the 1940s. At that time it was against the law for the manufacturer to add yellow color. Someone might think it was butter. A little packet of yellow coloring came with the oleomargarine, and the buyer could add the coloring. Having tasted both, I do not know how anyone could consider that the oleomargarine was real butter.

Milk is a valuable commodity. If you check the price per gallon, it's usually greater than the price of a gallon of gasoline. Back then we had plenty of milk, since we had a milk cow. Some of our relatives, who lived in town, did not have a milk cow. They could not afford to buy milk very often. One evening we had some of our urban relatives out for supper.

When they arrived, I was out milking Pet. I brought the milk in and set it on the table. That completed my adult function for the evening, and it was time to play with my cousins. I got out a toy frog. I could press the frog down, walk off, and in a minute or so it would leap. I flashed it to one of my cousins, told him to watch, pressed it down, and walked off. With my cousin watching the frog, and as Momma was picking up the milk bucket to go strain it, and my aunt was getting in the way, the frog leapt into the milk bucket. Momma was all for throwing the milk out because no one knew where that frog had been. I knew, but I was not telling. Aunt Eva would not hear about throwing that valuable two-and-a-half gallons of milk out. After considerable discussion, Aunt Eva took the milk home. Apparently the frog had not contaminated the milk too badly because none of them died, or for that matter, none of them got sick from drinking the milk. After that, I was not allowed to play with my frog when there was food on the table.

At about the same time Magnesia was born, I bought a Guernsey bull calf and named him Pluto. Shortly, I learned that two calves are more than twice as hard to raise as one calf. Pluto developed a bad case of mange. Charlie, a man from the poor farm (so he said), told me that the best cure for mange was to mix equal parts sulfur and crankcase oil and then add enough kerosene to make a workable paste. The "cure" was to be smeared on once a day. Pluto liked the cure as little as I liked applying it. Either the cure worked or the mange ran its course; anyway, Pluto recovered.

Animals I Have Hated

We didn't have enough feed in the pasture for all the cattle during the drought of the 1950s, so we started staking Magnesia (Maggie, for short) out each day after school. Being a pet, she had no fear of her boy and would not be led to or from the staking area. My mother helped, but Maggie would drag us both. Many were the days that I understood Uncle Carlos' hollering at Prince, but I had to keep my mouth shut. My mother was present, and she was known to wash bad words from one's mouth with Lifebuoy Soap. Papa thought it was time for me to start learning the scientific names of animals and suggested that whenever I was tempted to use Uncle Carlos' phrase, I should say the scientific name of an animal. It worked, and Momma never washed my mouth out for saying *Crotaluas atrox*. But more than once she asked, "Where?" That is the Latin name for the western diamondback rattlesnake. Maggie knew where she was going, so we should have just let her run.

Finally the day came when we did not have enough feed to feed Pet, so Papa sold her to Uncle Carlos as a dry cow. A few months later she had twins. While the rest of us griped about how Uncle Carlos got the best of the deal, my mother stated that we got a good price for a dry cow, and we sold Pet as a dry cow, so the deal was a good one. Momma never did look back and second-guess her decisions, and she expected us to do the same thing.

The Good Old Days

A message about the good old days at Brushy Creek was drummed into my head every time the TV was turned on. "These are the good old days at Brushy Creek. I kinda wish I was a kid again." This was Austin, Texas, in the early 1970s. Let me tell you what the good old days were really like.

When I was eleven years old, we were in the middle of a South Texas drought. The previous year the crop had failed. Papa had been a full-time farmer, but needed more income, so without downsizing the farm, he took over management of a mineral processing plant. As a result, I ended up with many chores. We had no money. The money Papa brought home went into trying to save our farm. The only food we had was what we could grow. We had a kitchen garden, about a half-acre in size. The only way we could grow anything was to haul water to it. That was one of my jobs. Before school and after school I fired up the tractor and took two fifty-five-gallon barrels down to the canal, filled them, and brought them back and watered the garden.

One Saturday in May, we were going to can beets. The night before, we washed jars and got prepared. The alarm went off long before daylight. As we got up and looked out into the garden, we saw Uncle Carlos' hogs in the beets. Uncle Carlos lived one-fourth mile down the road and seldom mended his fences. Momma was mad. She grabbed a hoe and took out after those hogs. She should have been on the track team. They made a beeline for a hole in the fence. She caught up with the last one just before it went through the hole. With a full downward swing, as if she was trying to set a

Animals I Have Hated

twenty-four-inch stake in one blow, she hit that hog on the back. That 300-pound hog fell over, as if dead.

If I can't can beets today, we will eat pork.

I turned to Papa and said, "Looks like we will be butchering a hog today rather than canning beets." Momma rested on the hoe and then got ready to hit the hog again. Just before the second blow fell, the seemingly-dead hog managed to crawl through a hole in the fence. Papa commented, "Hog got kinda hot, didn't it?" We missed out on beets that year, but we did have a good crop of mesquite beans and prickly pear. We had to wait three months

The Good Old Days

before we got a chance to butcher that hog; and when we did, the circumstances were rather strange.

Uncle Carlos came over one Saturday morning in August and said, "We gotta butcher a hog this morning." Papa looked up at him and said, "It's kinda hot." Uncle Carlos said, "Ah know, but we don't have no choice. The hogs got out, and I run one to death. It must have got too hot." We climbed into Uncle Carlos' pickup and tied the door shut with a rope. (Uncle Carlos was rich; he had a pickup.) We spent the morning butchering that hog. Papa noted that there were three parallel holes passing through the hog. They started in the middle of the back and moved down and forward. Papa winked at me, but he didn't say anything. Uncle Carlos didn't, either. Later Papa told Momma that the hog got overheated when Uncle Carlos chased it with a pitchfork in his hand.

Author's Note: *Hogs do not have sweat glands, so they can easily become over-heated. Wallowing around in the mud is a way of cooling off.*

Author's Note: *A pitchfork is a long-handled tool that resembles a dinner fork, but is about five-and-a-half to six feet long and usually has a wooden handle. The "fork" consists of three to six ten-inch-long metal tines that are sharpened. The pitchfork was designed so a farmer could pick up loose hay and stack it in a pile or on a wagon. Over the years we all found creative ways to use a pitchfork, including harvesting potatoes, and apparently Uncle Carlos found it could be used for chasing hogs.*

That winter we did not have enough feed for the chickens, and they could not find enough to keep going, so we butchered most of the flock. We were forced to spend what little money we had to buy chicken feed, so we could save our remaining stock and have a few eggs. Some animal kept getting into the chicken feed and eating five or ten pounds every night. Considering that the chicken feed cost five cents a pound, we just could not afford the loss.

During the night of the full moon, I heard a noise and got out of bed to investigate. I saw Momma slip out the back door with her broom. Quietly I slipped up to the back door and looked out. There stood a horse. It was wedged between the house and the car, and it was eating our chicken feed. Momma was standing right behind the horse, winding up with her broom. My first thought was, "She'll kill it, and then I'll have to drag it out and bury it." The broom came down on the horse's rump. In later years, I concluded that the horse could have done one of several things when it was hit by the broom. First, it could have kicked. Second, it could have backed out. Third, it could have stood there and taken a beating. Or fourth, it could have jumped over the hood of the car. The horse took the latter course of action. At breakfast Papa said, "Appears things got kinda hot for that horse."

Those were the good old days. They were so good that when Jimmy graduated from high school, he left home to go to diesel mechanics school and supported himself with a non-farm job. Bill didn't even wait to finish high school before he entered the Air Force. Papa was already working for Pozzolana, Inc., and he gradually phased out his farming operation. I decided to go to college. Nancy couldn't wait to follow in my footsteps. Mary, the baby, who was not exposed to the good old days, talked her husband into buying a woodstove and dreamed of buying a milk cow.

If the good old days are still alive at Brushy Creek, you'll never find me visiting Mary if she buys a house there. Actually, she never did, and she never bought a milk cow. They did have a wood stove for a while, but ended up getting rid of it. I guess she grew up.

The Good Old Days

Fighter

C hickens develop a pecking order, but they can't seem to count over thirty, since the strongest pecking orders are developed in flocks of less than thirty. Years ago, we purchased twenty-five white leghorn cockerels. Don't ask me why; maybe they were cheap.

Author's Note: P*rior to the development of hybrid chickens, white leghorns were the most popular breed of egg-laying chicken. All varieties of chickens laid eggs, but chickens were commonly divided into meat chickens, egg-laying chickens, and dual-purpose chickens. A good white leghorn hen would lay over three hundred eggs per year with the minimal amount of food. They were egg-producing machines. They carried very little meat on their skeletons. The cockerels, or males, did not lay eggs and were scrawny. Most hatcheries would sex the day-old white leghorn chicks and sell the pullets (females) to people who wanted egg production. I do not know what usually became of millions of white leghorn cockerels that were hatched every year, for I seldom saw them offered for sale.*

As our twenty-five white leghorn cockerels grew, one of them started to attack Jimmy whenever he went into the yard. Since Jimmy wouldn't fight back, Momma butchered the villain and cooked it. There was not enough meat on the bird even for two-year-old Jimmy. The next day, another young cock attacked Jimmy. When he entered the cook pot, a third took its place. This continued until all were eaten.

When radical Islamists replaced the Shah of Iran, I commented to Papa that maybe we should just Nuke that entire country. His only comment was, "Remember those white leghorn cockerels."

When Jimmy was in high school, we bought some Rhode Island Red chickens. These were dual-purpose chickens. While they did not lay as well as white leghorns, they had enough meat on their carcasses to make a nice meal. We ate all of the roosters except one that we named Fighter. He was a pet. When we were outside, he would come and join us. If we investigated something, he was right there helping us investigate. We all loved him, that is, all except for Mary. Mary, a preschooler, would take Nancy's Tonette and blow it at Fighter.

Author's Note: *A Tonette is a musical instrument that was commonly used in the schools. At that time most were made from Bakelite plastic and had eight holes on the top and one on the bottom. By either covering a hole or leaving it open, different notes could be played.*

Fighter would respond by attacking. Mary claimed she blew the Tonette at Fighter because he attacked her. This I could not accept, since Fighter was so lovable.

After several weeks, Mary quit going outside, because Fighter would be waiting for her. One Saturday, we had roast chicken. We boys compared notes on size, and then we asked Momma which hen she had butchered. She said, "Fighter." We left the table and went to investigate. Fighter was gone. Mary enjoyed eating Fighter; but each time I took a bite, the meat seemed to grow in my mouth. For years we continued to raise chickens, but we didn't have another rooster around. After all, no ordinary rooster could replace a friend like Fighter.

Fighter

Old Yowler

O ld Yowler, a forty-pound yellow cur, belonged to Imelda, who was a year ahead of me in school. Imelda was brilliant. To find out, all you had to do was ask her and she would tell you. She was also hardheaded and had the ability to multi-task. She could interfere in three conversations at the same time and try to run the lives of all her acquaintances. One afternoon, I caught Old Yowler in the act of raiding my rabbit pen. With a half-eaten rabbit as well as blood and fur in and around Old Yowler's mouth, I thought I had a case. After showing Imelda the evidence and making my accusations, she said, "That's not true. Old Yowler doesn't eat raw meat."

Later that year we stood in line at the school cafeteria to receive our lunches. As was her usual habit, she cut in line ahead of me. That day, lunch was to be fried chicken, so I talked about how they were serving us dead chicken. When she got her tray, she picked up her dead chicken and deposited it on my plate with the comment, "If you like dead chicken, you can eat dead chicken." Suddenly I liked Imelda more than I had ever liked her before. Not much better, but better. It was not until years later that it occurred to me that the reason she cut in front of a younger kid and ate lunch with him was she did not have any friends of her own age. I should have been helping her make friends rather than resenting her. Momma had told me this repeatedly, but it just did not sink in.

Animals I Have Hated

Rattlesnakes in Camp

When land is irrigated, rattlesnakes tend to disappear. During the 1940s Papa farmed near our home in Edinburg, south of McAllen on Depot Road, and north of Edinburg in the Redlands. The Redlands were not irrigated, so it was not uncommon to see rattlesnakes. Since the Redlands farm was about twenty miles north of Edinburg, a crew of three or four workers would camp out. The camp consisted of a tent made from Luna cloth, and a fire. There were cots in the tent, so snakes, tarantulas, and scorpions could not crawl into bed with the crew. We would take out supplies every week. They would furnish a list of needed supplies for us to bring out next week. It was lonely work, and after work there was no place to go for entertainment.

I told you we had lots of rattlesnakes.

We drove up to the Redlands farm camp and got out. One of the crew grabbed a gunny sack, untied it, and shook it. Rattlesnakes spilled all over the campsite. Papa pointed to the tractor and told me to get on it, and then assessed the situation. Antonio said in rapid-fire Spanish what could loosely be translated as, "See, I told you we had lots of rattlesnakes around the camp." The rattlesnakes chose not to stay around camp, and before long I got down off the tractor. Supplies were unloaded, fields were examined, reports were received, and instructions were given. Antonio gave Papa a list of things that would be needed the following week.

The next week when we arrived at the camp with supplies that had been ordered the week before, Antonio said they were out of "gasoline" and several other things. Papa wanted to know why he had not put them on the list the previous week. Antonio explained that they were not out of those particular supplies the previous week. Afterwards, Papa did the inventory each week. When I asked him about it, he said some people can plan and some people live in the present.

These were not the only rattlesnakes we dealt with over the years. Here are a few other times they crossed our paths.

At Pozzolana, Inc., we pumped water from a pond near the road to a concrete tank on a hilltop. This gave us the water pressure needed to run the plant. Periodically someone had to go up and check the water level in the concrete tank. If the tank was full, we would cut the pump off. Ramón went up, and about fifteen minutes later he came back with a string of rattles off of what must have been a very large rattlesnake. An hour and a half later I went up to check the water level. Crawling down the road was a six-foot rattlesnake. Its rattles had been freshly cut off. I pitched the snake in the back of the pickup; and when I returned to the plant, I called everybody together and told them how brave Ramón was. After the snake was taken care of, Ramón was rather pale and looked as if he might get sick.

Animals I Have Hated

Back when I was going to college, there were not any student loans or Pell grants. My parents could not afford to help financially, so I had to earn money in order to stay in school. One of the ways I earned money was catching rattlesnakes with a friend. We would ship them off to a place in Narco, Louisiana, and we would be paid a handsome price of fifty cents a pound. Even though I saw some six-foot rattlesnakes, I never saw a ten-pound rattlesnake. If we had an injured rattlesnake, we would decapitate it and dissect the head out to show the poison sacs and the bud fangs. A dissected head brought much more than a live snake. We would normally filet the snake and cook it. I was processing a snake, and my partner, Earl, picked up the snake head which I had dropped in a jar of alcohol, took it inside, and sitting at his dining room table, started dissecting. His wife was cooking supper. He was holding the head with a pair of long-handled tweezers. The head flinched, slid down the tweezers, and injected venom into his thumb. He said to his wife in a calm voice, "The snake bit me, and I need to go to the hospital." She responded in just as calm a voice, "Use your shoelace as a tourniquet, and go get into the car. I'll drive you to the hospital." He did, so she did. It was not until they got to the hospital, which was only a few blocks away, that she realized he was really snake-bit.

While he was recovering, he promised his wife that he would give up snake hunting. At the same time I promised a young lady whom I was dating that I would give up snake hunting. I packed all of our snakes up and shipped them off, and had the place pretty well cleaned up by the time Earl got out of the hospital. Within two weeks he was back catching rattlesnakes. Even though I quit going with that young lady within a few months, for the last fifty years I have kept my promise to her. I'm sure my wife appreciates that. I lost track of Earl, and then recently I saw a story on TV about a man who had been bitten by a very venomous African snake. That was Earl. Earl became a herpetologist of some note. While he taught school, and he was a wonderful teacher, he was also involved in importing and distributing reptiles from all over the world. After making contact with Earl and wishing him a speedy recovery, he sent me ten dollars that he owed me from when we were in the rattlesnake business.

While we were actively catching snakes, Dr. Bradway asked for a large rattlesnake so she could dissect it for her comparative anatomy class. I furnished one about five feet long, and on the day of the dissection she anesthetized it with chloroform. She took it out of its container, rolled it on its back, added props so it would remain stable, and started an incision. When the incision was less than two inches long, the snake rolled over. She turned it back on its back, stabilized it, and started the incision again. The snake rolled over. She grabbed a-hold of it, it rattled, she let go of it, and it crawled off the table. I was summoned to the Comparative Anatomy Lab. There were no students, lab assistants, or professors in the lab. Even though there wasn't much of a crack under the door, there was a towel in place to keep the rattlesnake from getting out. I was asked to go in and retrieve the snake, which by this time was in hiding. It took only fifteen or twenty minutes to find the snake and capture it. Dr. Bradway then decided to do a dissection of a dead rattlesnake.

Here is another interaction I had with a snake.

There is a nursery rhyme about girls being sugar and spice and everything nice and how boys are snips and snails and puppy dog tails. There is a certain amount of truth in the rhyme. I firmly believe that girls grow up to become ladies, and boys grow up to become bigger boys. Yes, there are those who will disagree with this premise vehemently and tell me that I do not know girls and ladies, but I'm telling the story, so that is the way it is going to be told. A group of us were camping. This was not just any camping trip; this was a scientific expedition. We were monitoring the temperature of eggs in the nest of a Least Grebe. No, we didn't use a mercury thermometer; we had installed a fake egg in the nest that contained a thermocouple. We ran thermocouple wire to an instrument that would remotely measure the temperature once per hour. We were doing this around the clock. There were three of us on the team. It took only one person to take the reading and record it; a second person was there to make sure the person taking the reading did not fall asleep. The third person normally would be sleeping in preparation for taking over duties later on. In this day and time, using a little device called a HOBO, we could remotely measure the egg temperature every few seconds for three years and never have to worry about reading an instrument until we were through, but we were dealing with state-of-the-art equipment from before the electronic age. This was back before color television. This is that age referred to by some people as "the dark ages."

I was sleeping and periodically listening to my two companions talk. They were plotting something, but I wasn't sure what it was. In due time I felt the smooth skin of a large snake move past my cheek and into my sleeping bag, and I heard a muffled chuckle or two. The snake appeared to be a long one, probably over six feet long. The skin was smooth, so obviously it was not a rattlesnake. Considering the snake's length, it was probably an indigo snake, and they were expecting me to be terrified, thinking that a rattlesnake had joined me in my sleeping bag. I went back to sleep. Over the next hour or so I would hear comments from over by the fire wondering when I was going to notice the snake in my sleeping bag, and wondering how loud I would scream when I noticed the snake. About 3 AM it was time for one of them to wake me up so I could start my shift. I slid out of my sleeping bag, being careful not to disturb the snake. While drinking a cup of coffee, one of them wondered if I'd had any visitors during the night. I responded that yes, a snake had joined me for warmth, and since he was not causing any trouble, I let him stay. I suggested that my companion who was about to take a nap move the snake to his sleeping bag so it could stay warm. "But it might be a rattlesnake." I responded that it wasn't, that it was an indigo snake. I was asked if I had looked at

Barn Owls

it. I had not, so they wanted to know how I knew. With a grin, I said, "I stayed awake in class and listened."

I wonder if now, over fifty years later, they're still pulling teenage-type practical jokes and thinking that they're funny.

Back in the 1960s I had the opportunity to do a Grand Tour. Not a European Grand Tour that was common with up-and-coming young gentlemen back in the 1920s, but of Southeast Asia. Our federal government was nice enough to make all of the travel arrangements and provide me with things to do while I was there. They even paid me a salary. During this time I had an opportunity to spend time in some remote villages and deep in some dark jungles. One of the things I learned in the villages was that cobras, one of the most deadly snakes on this planet, were welcome guests in homes. They came in and eliminated rats. As long as the occupants of the home did not bother the cobras or step on them, the cobras did not bother them. I was present in one home when a cobra came through the room we were in. Even though I knew that it would not do any harm, I suspect my heart rate increased while it was in the room. When I was out in the jungle, I saw wildlife from time to time. Among other things I saw a few cobras. While others wanted to kill the cobras, I was against it. Their explanations ranged from "the cobras might kill someone," to "we want a trophy." My explanation was simple; the villagers welcome the cobras because they eliminate rats; if we kill the cobras, we are doing them a disservice. If we leave the cobras, the villagers are much more likely to be friendly to us than if we kill their live rat traps. I don't think I ever convinced anybody, but I saved a few cobras, because while I talked, the cobras slithered away. Anyway, the experience taught me that all of God's creatures have a place and what some consider a scourge, can actually be a blessing in disguise.

Barn Owls

One summer Jesse Huff and I found a barn owl nest under a loading ramp at one of Rio Clay Products' remote clay pits in Starr County, Texas. Being young gentlemen with an appreciation for wildlife in a cage, we each ended up with two owlets. While I don't remember what happened to Jesse's, I remember mine. To begin with, I gave them cheerful names: Mordecai and Ichabod. The name Mordecai comes from the Book of Esther, where he was an honorable servant of the king and Esther's father. Ichabod, of course, comes from Ichabod Crane, a fictional character in Washington Irving's short story, The Legend of Sleepy Hollow.

To keep the owls caged, I built a cage, thirty inches on edge, from half-inch hardware cloth. Feeding was not a problem; they would take anything handed them. Food usually consisted of hamburger, sparrows, meat scraps, fingers, and hands.

We did not have an air conditioner, so during the warm months of the year, the family would adjourn to the backyard each evening. Normally all of our free-roaming animals would join us. After Mordecai and Ichabod joined the family, I would release them each evening so they could visit the human members of their family. We found that they were curious.

The cats quickly realized that owls were birds. The stalk was on. For a week or more, I valiantly rescued the owls before the cats pounced. After the owls could fly, I let them take care of themselves. Usually they would seem to ignore the stalking cats. When a cat pounced at an owl, the owl would hop to one side.

One evening Mordecai flew around the yard, then landed about four feet behind Sylvester (Nancy's black-and-white tomcat that Uncle Zara gave her, which turned out to be a brindle female). Quietly, Mordecai stalked Sylvester. After a three-minute stalk, Mordecai grabbed Sylvester's tail with his beak. Sylvester lit out like she had business in the next county. Within a day or two, the cats and the owls were stalking each other on a regular basis. The owls always landed and walked up on the cats.

If she will just flick her tail, I can grab it.

We were highly entertained for several weeks, but as the owls grew, the cats started getting the worst of the game. By the time the owls were four months old, the cats retreated under the house when the owls were out. Both owls would stare at anyone who approached them. One evening Papa walked up to Mordecai and then proceeded to walk around him. Mordecai's head followed

Animals I Have Hated

Papa's movements—one revolution of the head, then two revolutions of the head, finally three revolutions of the head. I begged
Papa to stop, because I didn't want to have to watch Mordecai
wring his own neck. Papa said, "Watch. When he gets his head just
past straight back, he turns it around so fast his head blurs." I
watched and was relieved to see the blur of a rapidly-turning head.

Periodically I couldn't catch the owls to put them away, so they
would spend the night out. When they were about six months old,
they were gone for three nights and then returned. Shortly thereafter, they disappeared.

Author's Note*: Our land was irrigated. That meant that a series of
canals were connected to a pumping station on the Rio Grande
River. The pumps ran twenty-four hours a day. Water was ordered, and then the ditch rider was responsible for getting it to
the farmer who ordered it and ensuring that the farmer did not
get more than he was allotted. Water flowed day and night, and
the farmer had to be ready to take the water whenever it arrived, even if it arrived at 2:00 am. During the irrigation season,
we always had kerosene lanterns filled and ready to light if they
were needed.*

Early the next summer, while irrigating a field near our house,
I saw a barn owl circle, and then land on a dike about twenty feet
from me. After remaining for a few minutes, he flew into the night.
I wonder, was that Mordecai or Ichabod?

Guineas & Rocks

A neighbor obtained a few guineas, some white and some pearled. In due time, they crossed and produced splashed guineas (pearled with white splashes). The neighbor moved and abandoned his guineas. This didn't seem to bother the guineas. They developed a range of about half a mile in diameter, which included our home and Uncle Carlos' home.

As months passed and we listened to their song, "Pa-trot, Pa-trot" and "Cha, Cha, Cha," we often discussed separating them from their lives and eating them. If we were going to eat guinea, I would tell Papa, we should use the traditional recipe, which involves placing a dressed guinea in a pressure cooker with an igneous rock and cooking it at fifteen pounds pressure for three days and three nights. After the pressure drops, you throw the guinea away and eat the rock. He would then comment on spices and seasonings.

Several months later, Dog, my good-for-nothing mutt with an original name (who ever heard of a dog named Dog?), inadvertently caught and killed a guinea. Since it was too tough for Dog to eat, he brought it to me. I dressed the guinea and took it to my mother. Three days later, when Papa and I returned from a fishing trip, my mother was dropping the pressure on the pressure cooker. When we sat down to supper, she served us an igneous rock about the size of that guinea.

Guineas are known for their ability to hide their nests well, incubate their eggs well, and then expect their chicks (the correct word is keets, but then I would have to explain what a keet was) to be able to keep up with them. This exposes the chicks to predation, getting wet, and getting left behind. As a result, guineas do not raise as large a percentage of their chicks that hatch as chicken hens do. This tends to keep the population under control. Only the fittest survive.

A tender guinea hen for supper?

A number of years passed, and we were living in Knippa, Texas. We had a few different barnyard fowl, and I decided to get some guineas. I fed them so they would come up and eat within a few feet of me, but as with all guineas, they were still wild birds. About that time I purchased an incubator so that I could hatch eggs. When I found a guinea nest, I would put the eggs in the incubator and hatch them. Then I would raise the guineas in a confined space until they were about half-grown. My flock grew. One of the guineas had problems eating. When I would feed the guineas, it would not get its fair share. I started holding food in my hand for it, and it started eating from my hand. When other guineas started to follow the practice, I would hold my hand close to a knee, and the guinea would sit on my knee while it ate from my hand.

Soon the entire flock wanted to eat from my hand. I could go out, sit in a chair, and soon I would have guineas on my head, on my shoulders, in my lap, any place they could get. Never before or since have I seen such a large flock of tame guineas. I'm sure they exist; I just have never seen them. By the way, guineas have an unpleasant body odor.

When I told Momma about my tame flock of guineas, she said, "They must be male guineas. Just about every woman knows that the way to a man's heart is through his stomach." She then laughed and said, "Seriously, if you want to influence someone, you need to find out what is important to him, and then provide it."

Obviously, years before she felt that an igneous rock cooked with a guinea was important to me, so she provided it. It was.

Oddie's Chickens

Heinrich Adolph Hitler Schmitt emigrated from Germany to Edinburg, Texas, after WWII as a displaced person. He was about eleven and was accompanied by his mother, sister, two older brothers, and a younger brother. The family was sponsored by the Lutheran Church in Edinburg. Uncle Carlos, the farmer down the road who owned a pickup, provided housing for the family and employment for the oldest son as a tractor driver.

Heinrich insisted on calling himself Adolph; however, his family called him Oddie, so his friends adopted that name for him. While he insisted that Hitler was his third name, his mother denied it. Our relationship went through several stages. I had him convinced that if he got out of line, I would beat the tar out of him. After putting up with this for six months, we had our one and only fight. After that, I knew that if I got out of line, he would beat the tar out of me.

Notwithstanding the pecking order, Oddie took an interest in my activities and projects. After becoming acquainted with my activities and projects, he would either inform me about how much better it was done in Germany or outdo me himself. I planted zinnias, so he planted dahlias. Mine were good-looking, but his looked like a garden catalog advertisement. When I was twelve, I saved my cotton-chopping money and bought a chicken coop that was eight feet long and eight feet wide for thirty-five dollars and fenced in as much land as one hundred and sixty-five feet of fencing covered. Chicken wire came in rolls that were one hundred and sixty-five feet long. Fence posts were scrounged, and one-by-four bottom boards were added to keep the chickens in. After a short time, I was selling fryers, and several months later I was selling eggs to HEB, the local grocery store.

Oddie watched my progress and then converted an existing hog pen to a chicken coop and fenced as large a yard as one hundred and sixty-five feet of fencing could cover. He kidded me about keeping my hens penned in and feeding them expensive laying mash. He said that he turned loose any hens that wouldn't lay that day so they could fend for themselves. I pondered the matter and finally got out Papa's 1936 Feathered World Almanac. "The Book" told how to separate good layers from poor layers, but it didn't tell how to check whether a hen would lay an egg that day.

Before school one day, I arrived at Oddie's chicken pen while he was doing chores. He caught each hen and inserted a finger. If he didn't feel an egg, he placed the hen outside the pen. This provided me with yet another example of how there is much knowledge in the world that is not in books, and that we should try to learn from everyone we are in contact with. However, that was one of the things I would prefer to learn from a book.

Even though laying mash cost five cents a pound, I continued feeding all my hens laying mash.

Animals I Have Hated

Fluffy

Uncle Zara was at it again. He was holding a young, yellow, long-haired kitten out to five-year-old Mary and declaring, "It's a little boy, so your momma won't object to you having it." Momma did object to having fourteen cats, but objecting didn't help much. The only bright spot was that when we arrived at fourteen cats, they always started dying off.

Mary brought the kitten home and named it Fluffy. I told her that Fluffy wasn't a good name for a cat. She told me that Dog wasn't a good name for a dog. Everywhere Mary went, she carried Fluffy. I even worried that Fluffy would forget how to walk. All the while, Mary talked to Fluffy and instructed her on the important things in life (to Mary).

Under the table, near my place, a knot had fallen from a floorboard. Papa, many years before, had nailed a can lid over the hole, but the can lid had finally worn out. Whenever I dropped any food, I would ease it to the hole with a toe and then push it through. Fluffy found the hole while we were eating supper one evening. My first inkling of it was when four claws penetrated my big toe to the bone and then tried to drag my big toe down the hole. Momma didn't think that losing a toe was an excuse to holler like a guinea at the supper table. Without knocking the table over, I barely managed to save my big toe. After that, I kept it out of reach of the hole. Thereafter, several times during each meal, a yellow paw and leg with long claws unsheathed would come through the hole, extend out about eight inches, and then make a circle with the hole as its center. If anything was encountered, it was drawn down the hole and eaten.

Mary regularly brought her vicious cat into the house. Each time, she would show the cat how to open the door. "You climb up the screen and grab the handle with this paw, and then press on the frame with this paw. The door will open, and you can slide in."Mary didn't listen when I told her that Fluffy was too stupid to learn. When I told her that the only way for a cat to get through a door was to slip through when someone opened the door, she would respond, "She might get her tail caught." One day Fluffy beat us to the table and sampled our supper. Mary swore she had left Fluffy outside. Fluffy was evicted; but before we could sit down, the door banged, and Fluffy was in the house. Thereafter, Fluffy had the run of the supper table, whether we wanted it or not.

Several cases of rabies occurred in our county, so a program was initiated to have all dogs vaccinated. Mary didn't want Fluffy to get rabies, so she convinced Momma to let her take Fluffy to be vaccinated. One cat among all those dogs could have caused problems, but for once Fluffy behaved.

The day after the vaccination, Fluffy ran a fever; the next day she wouldn't eat; the following day Fluffy died. It's awfully hard to explain to your pesky kid sister that the shot that was supposed to save the cat's life killed it.

Do You Want to Go Wading?

Leeches lived in the irrigation ditches across the lower Rio Grande Valley. Most of them were only a half-inch to an-inch-and-a-quarter long. They were not the monster five- and six-inch leeches I learned about while on my Grand Tour in Southeast Asia a few years later. While they would get on humans, unlike some other leeches they did not cut through the skin. Basically they were a harmless curiosity.

One of the upperclassman at Pan American College was study-ing leeches. He asked me if I knew where to find some leeches, and I assured him that I could give him as many as he needed. I then wanted to know how much he would be willing to pay me for some leeches. After negotiations that lasted several days, we agreed on fifty cents apiece.

I then went home and asked my younger sister, Mary, if she would like to go wading in the canal. She always loved to go wad-ing in the canal, but Momma insisted that she had to have somebody available with her to keep an eye on her. Her overbear-ing and spiteful brother was offering to be nice to her, so we headed off to the canal. I let her wade for about fifteen or twenty minutes and then suggested she get out of the water. I noticed some leeches, so I offered to pick them off. Since she did not like leeches, she let me. As I placed them in a jar, I counted them and determined that I did not have quite enough to fulfill my contract with the upperclassman.

So I asked Mary if she would like to wade a little longer. By this time she'd forgotten about the leeches, and she enjoyed another ten minutes of wading. I then asked her to get out, pointed out that she had gotten a few more leeches, and offered to pick them off.

After we got that taken care of, I walked her home. I was such a nice brother for a change.

Mary loved to wade in the irrigation canal.

Everything was peaceful until Mary told our sister Nancy how nice I had been. Nancy wanted to know what I was going to do with the leeches. I told her that they were helping pay for a college education. Nancy made a big deal over how I had used Mary in order to go out and make money. It was all my fault. If I would have pinched Mary after I got the leeches, she never would've told Nancy what a nice brother I was, and I would not have had to put up with Nancy's harassment.

The only thing harder than putting up with Nancy's harassment was having people tell me that I should spell leeches with a double e rather than an "ea." I'm a chemist, and leach is a very good word.

Animals I Have Hated

Pozzo's Pups

I was out at the Pozzolan Plant, helping Papa. Among other things, I looked at Pozzo's pups, petted each one, and looked at the ribbons tied on each pup. I asked Pa Barrett why the plant was called a pozzolan plant. He pointed to Pozzo and stated that the plant was named after her. That made sense to me, and I accepted it for a few months. When I started having a greater understanding of what was going on, I knew that I'd been had.

Author's Note: *The Bureau of Reclamation had come to the Lower Rio Grande Valley of Texas to find a sucker to process volcanic ash so that the finished product could be used as a pozzolan in Falcon Dam. A relative of mine ended up being the sucker. When the job was too much for him, he called Papa in to solve the problems, which Papa did. The Romans originally used volcanic ash from near the town of Pozzuoli near Mt. Vesuvius, to make mortar stucco and concrete by mixing it with lime putty, so the product was called Pozzolan, and the dog had been named for the plant, not the other way around. Now just a little bit of chemistry. When Portland cement hydrates, hydrated lime is given off which will eventually lead to the degradation of the product. Pozzolan is added to react with that hydrated lime and form more cement binder. The reaction absorbs energy, so the concrete does not get as hot as it cures. It makes a better and cheaper concrete. While technically we were on the cutting edge of Bronze Age technology, it sure sounds better to claim we were on the cutting edge of Stone Age technology.*

The reason that Pozzo was so popular with the workers was that some of the workers did not have all of the paperwork to be in the country legally. Border Patrol agents would periodically make a raid, and the only thing that Pozzo hated was Border Patrol agents. She could detect them a mile away. When she started barking, the crew would drift off into the brush, and there were no illegals around when the Border Patrol arrived. Those of us who were legal would make necessary adjustments so the plant could idle with minimal oversight, and then, as soon as an agent saw us, we would dash into the brush with the Border Patrol in pursuit. Whenever Pozzo had pups, the various workers would put ribbons on the different pups when they were as little as a few days old. This established ownership. I don't know if any of Pozzo's pups were ever half as good as she was.

Pozzo and her pups

Pozzo was not the only plant dog that I have known. Every plant used to have one or more plant dogs, but with modern safety rules, plant dogs are not as common as they used to be. In fact, the federal Mine Safety and Health Administration rules state that if a dog shows up on a work site, the supervisor should stand between the dog and the workers and state, "This is a dog. Dogs can bite. Stay away from this dog and any other dog that comes onto the plant site." Can you picture a supervisor doing that?

I met one memorable dog about ten years ago at a Mexican plant. For whatever reason, I was selected to serve on my company's acquisition team to determine whether to buy a manufacturing plant in Mexico. My area of expertise on the team was cement technology. There were others who understood quality control, marketing, cost analysis, finance, etc. In all, there were eight of us. The attorney who was giving us a tour was very concerned that we might learn something that would kill the deal. I kept wandering away from the group and asking questions. He would come and herd me back to the group; and when I would ask him a question, the response would be, "The person who could answer that question is Señor _____, and he is not here now." I was getting upset with the runaround. The plant dog was large and hobbled on three legs, because one of the hind legs had been broken several years before and it had not healed correctly. One of the workers told me that a forklift had run over the dog. The workers fed him, and all he really wanted out of life was some love from a human. He would approach one person after another and lean against them in hopes of a little petting and a kind word. As the attorney was dragging me back to the group for about the seventh or eighth time, the dog had approached Russell, a member of the team. Russell knelt down, petted the dog, and talked to him. Watching them, it appeared that they loved each other.

I pointed out the pair to the attorney and commented that Russell was having all sorts of problems with the business deal, and you could see that he had abandoned even looking at his area of expertise, so that he could communicate with the dog. The attorney wanted to know what he could do to get Russell back on board. I suggested that since Russell loved that dog, if he boxed the dog up and shipped him to Russell's home in Georgia, Russell would forget about his reservations. The attorney proceeded to tell

Russell that he would ship the dog to his home, when it suddenly dawned on the attorney that a hoax had been pulled on him. He knew that his plan had failed, but he made the best of it.

He relaxed, allowed us to ask questions, and then made a serious attempt to answer the questions. When I would wander off and talk to the employees, he would herd the group along behind me and made no attempt to interfere with my quest for knowledge. Meanwhile, Russell and the dog were inseparable. Based on what I learned from the employees, I recommended that we purchase the plant, and the other team members agreed, so, much to the attorney's surprise, the company bought the plant.

Sanforized Skunk

W hile in the upper elementary grades, I had a denim work jacket. The label said several things, including "Sanforized Skunk."

Author's Note: *For those of you who are too young to remember the good old days, the first time most clothes were washed, they shrank. The only way to prevent this was for the manufacturer to put the cloth through a process called Sanforization. The tag in the clothes included the words "Sanforized Shrunk." Young ladies loved for their mothers to buy jeans for them that were not Sanforized. They would put them on and then get in the backyard and hose themselves down. This led to form-fitting, skin-tight jeans. After that first "washing," the jeans maintained the same size with further washings. In most high schools, Fridays were dress-down days, and the young ladies would wear their skin-tight jeans. The question I had, but never had the nerve to ask was: How did they get them buttoned? Chemistry and Physics teachers taught the concept that one cannot put more into a container than the container can hold, but they never tried to get that point across on Fridays.*

In due time, I outgrew the jacket, and Nancy inherited it. She liked it as much as I did, so I pointed out the "Sanforized Skunk." She insisted that it said "Sanforized Shrunk." Nancy started a sibling war over the "Sanforized Skunk" and hotly waged it against me, until Mary inherited the jacket three years later. Mary didn't mind wearing a "Sanforized Skunk." In fact, I think she enjoyed wearing that Sanforized Skunk.

The Sanforized Skunk

I must compliment both of my sisters, since neither attempted to wear skin-tight jeans. At that time we had one indoor bathroom, and I'm sure we would never have made it to school on time if one of them had had to stuff herself into jeans that were three sizes too small to be comfortable.

The Deer Slayer

Each year the Senator leased a tract of land in northern Starr County for deer hunting. He took clients hunting there, so that expenses could be considered business expenses. Papa, who was one of the Senator's brothers, would usually be invited along to hunt, to tend camp, and to ensure that there were no surprises. Of course, one of us boys tagged along. He never took two of us at the same time. When we suggested it, he would grin and say, "One boy, half a man; two boys, nothing."

Certain aspects of the hunt could always be predicted–such as Papa sighting-in his rifle, an old forty-four-fifty.

Author's Note: *The forty-four refers to the caliber of the rifle. The bore or hole in the barrel was forty-four hundredths inch in diameter. That is nearly half an inch in diameter. As an adult, I can stick the end of my little finger down the barrel. The second number refers to the grains of powder in the bullet—in this case, fifty grains. A grain is a unit of weight based on the average weight of a grain of wheat. In layman's terms, the rifle shot a big chuck of lead and propelled it with enough powder to kick hard.*

Three shots were required each year. He then placed the rifle under his cot, in case a deer walked into camp. (They did, but that is another story.) He would then help me sight-in a rifle—borrowed, of course. Being the lowest in the pecking order, I usually ended up with a rifle that had been abused. Rather than three shots into the bull's eye, it usually took six or eight. I did not like this, since cartridges were expensive. At night, I would dream about what I could do if I had a rifle as good as Papa's. I would not even have to hit a deer with it. The concussion would kill him if I hit within five feet of the deer.

When Papa was cooking, food was always good in camp. Even though Papa could not cook at home, he was a specialist over a mesquite fire. But then, maybe it was the business-expense steaks that were so good.

The Senator's rifle was his pride and joy. He even had a fancy cleaning kit. The pocket in the end of the stock that would normally contain a cleaning kit always contained three cartridges. Clients often asked him why. He told them that a person might need an extra round or two if he got lost. The cavity provided a convenient way to carry them. This made a good explanation, but I knew better. It happened when I was twelve. One evening in camp, the men, all except Papa, fought the black bear (Oso Negro).

Author's Note: *Oso Negro is a Mexican brand of an alcoholic beverage containing vodka and gin. It contains about thirty-eight percent alcohol. Oso Negro is often mixed with orange juice to make a drink called a Screwdriver, or with tomato juice to make a Bloody Mary.*

This continued until after I went to bed, which was not early. The next morning I woke well before daylight to the smell of bacon and eggs over a mesquite fire. During the hearty breakfast, we discussed the possibilities of the morning's hunt. The Senator announced that he was going to a pasture about a half-mile from the camp. He had scouted out a stand of mesquite that would make a good blind. This was before the elevated blinds and deer feeders that are now common throughout South Texas came into use. By getting there forty-five minutes early and remaining quiet, he would be able to carefully select the best buck in the pasture and cleanly kill it. He announced that he would be back in camp by 9:00 AM. We each announced where we were going to hunt. Papa announced that he would put a stew on for lunch, since a norther had blown in overnight, and the temperature was down into the low forties.

Author's Note: *A norther is a winter storm that blows in, usually out of the north. During a south Texas winter, it is not uncommon for the temperature to be in the eighties during the day and when a norther blows in the temperature can drop into the forties in a matter of an hour or so.*

We each went our separate ways. As I hiked along, I marveled at the ability of the men to be up so early after fighting the black bear (Oso Negro) half of the night.

My stand was over a dry creek. In scouting it out, I had not found a single deer track within sight of it. But that was understandable. I was lowest in the pecking order. The best areas had to be reserved for the clients. Dawn pinkened the eastern sky. I knew a big buck was going to get lost and come stand in front of my blind. Soon I could see individual trees that were one hundred yards away. I heard a shot. It was from the Senator's direction, so I knew he had his buck. I was jubilant.

Thirty seconds later, another shot. He had two bucks. The Senator would not waste a shot. Thirty seconds later, a third shot. The Senator had three deer, but that was illegal. Even though he could probably talk his way out of the consequences for breaking the law, it might be a distress signal. As I eased out of my blind to go help the Senator, I spooked a buck that was not supposed to be there. Since the Senator was in trouble, I did not stop to shoot. A fourth shot. That is odd. Distress signals are three shots. The Senator must really be in trouble. As I trotted down the trail to the Senator's aid, I heard a fifth, a sixth, and a seventh shot.

When I got to the pasture, several of the men were there. The Senator was cut and bruised, and the stock of his rifle was broken. There was what had been a beautiful ten-point buck on the ground. One antler was broken off. Listening to the conversation, I quickly determined that the Senator had shot the buck seven times. The buck was still alive, so he hit it over the head with his rifle and broke the stock. Apparently the buck had a lot of fight left in him when the Senator started swinging his rifle. Cousin Alvin and I were left to field-dress the buck and transport it back to camp. He pointed out to me that the Senator must have missed several times for the buck to be alive after seven shots. We looked it over, top and bottom, front and back, left and right, and concluded that the Senator had suffered from that fight with the black bear (Oso Negro) more than we thought. Since we wanted to be invited back, we swore each other to secrecy. The only marks on that magnificent buck were the marks inflicted by the stock of the Senator's rifle and a nick on an antler inflicted by a bullet. After that, the Senator started carrying three extra cartridges to dispatch any deer that was not quite dead.

Several years later, while hunting, Cousin Alvin and my brother Jimmy found two stray dogs. They were skin and bones and could barely stand, so the boys picked them up and carried them to camp. That year, the Senator had bought groceries. He went heavy on Spam. By the fourth day of the hunt, Spam was the only meat left. The Senator opened up a can of Spam and gave it to the dogs. They both refused to eat Spam. After expressing his displeasure at ungrateful dogs, he drove to Hebbronville and purchased food suitable for a starving dog. The Senator adopted one of the dogs, and Jimmy adopted the other and named it Brown Dog (a good name, since it was a brown dog).

One year, after I developed an interest in photography, I took my camera to hunting camp. That year I commented that the deer were so tame, one could almost feed them from one's hand. Even though I didn't shoot a deer, I took some good photos. Later, by using a technique known as rear screen projection (this was three or four decades before PhotoShop was invented), I was able to make a photo showing a deer from the hunting lease eating from my hand.

I don't know why, but the next year I wasn't invited. Nor was I invited the year after that. Maybe the Senator didn't want me to feed his deer.

Weimar

I n the early 1960s, what we thought was a Weimaraner pup wandered up to my parents' home east of La Puerta, Starr County, Texas.

Author's Note: La Puerta is Spanish for The Door. The unincorporated community is located on US Highway 83 about four miles southeast of Rio Grande City. At the time of this story the community consisted of ten to fifteen houses and Pedro Chapa's small store. The border crossing, for which the community was named, is about one-and-a-half-miles south on the Rio Grande River. The crossing was used for smuggling from the early days of Texas.

Instead of being gray and having gray eyes like a Weimaraner was supposed to be, she was rusty brown in color and had rust-brown eyes. Maybe she was a color variation of the Weimaraner breed that no one has ever heard of. Maybe she was a Hungarian Vizsla. She could have been a rust-brown color phase of a German Shorthair Pointer. While my parents tried to find the owner and hoped that she would leave, my sisters became attached to her. Since the owner did not show up, Weimar (we pronounced her name Wēēmer) was adopted into the family. In time she had a litter of twelve pups. At that point, Momma decided that before there was another batch, Weimar should be fixed. She was.

I thought Weimar could use some training, but I was in college and did not have the opportunity to provide it. My sisters were too softhearted to follow my instructions, so Weimar grew up without the manners which any dog ought to have. Now, Weimar was smart and would try anything once; and if she liked it, would continue.

One day she noticed Mary lying in a hammock. Since Weimar could not get into the hammock by herself, she lay down on the brick patio–on her back, of course. Later, someone put her into the hammock, and she was content to sleep in it on her back.

About a year after Weimar joined the family, a man showed up looking for a very valuable registered pup he had lost the previous year while quail hunting. He did not have much hope of finding it, but since he was back in the area quail hunting again, he thought he would ask around. I do not remember whom he talked to, but whoever it was could not help him because he did not refer to the Weimaraner breed, and immediately forgot the name of the breed he referred to. Weimar did not come out from under the house and reveal what the vet had done to this man's very valuable dog at Momma's request. We never saw the man again.

Weimar followed Mary out to pick fruit from the garden. If they were good enough for Mary, they were good enough for her, so she sampled some and liked them. We would see her out there from time to time eating grapes. After she had eaten all she could reach while on all fours, she would rear up on her hind legs and continue. This activity got Mary in trouble at school one day. Her English teacher asked the class to write a theme about some true incident or event they had experienced. Mary wrote about Weimar eating fruit off the trees and vines. The teacher didn't even bother to grade it, but wrote across the paper, "I said a true experience." Mary came home in tears. No one would believe what she wrote about her dog. She ended up writing another story about the family fighting over the hot rolls at the supper table. Papa always had the best chance of getting the last roll, 'cause he used his fork. I depended on speed and on kicking under the table, but I got caught by the tines from time to time. But this is getting away from the main theme of this story.

Mary had to have a project for the science fair one year, so she decided to demonstrate several methods for making carbon dioxide. One of the methods was to ferment grape juice, and the result was a quart of grape wine. Mary is very careful about not wasting anything, so she offered the wine to my parents; but they stated they were not interested. She offered it to me; but since I had stolen the last roll off her plate the last time I was home, I didn't trust her. She would have offered it to Nancy, but Nancy would have given her a lecture about drinking. She figured that she was too young to do the taste-testing, so she called Weimar. Weimar was not interested until Mary called Officer (a black cat that supervised everything). Officer was interested, so Weimar chased him away and licked the pan clean. Mary gave Weimar more. To make a long story short, Weimar got drunk. Not just a little drunk, but a lot of drunk. She slept some. Mary got worried about her dog and woke her up. Weimar would prance across the yard. She must have thought that she was three feet off the ground. Her hind legs would go faster than her front legs. Soon she would be traveling sideways. About that time, she would trip and roll. Never have I seen such a comical sight. All the while, Mary was feeling guilty because she had gotten her beloved dog drunk. Several days later, Weimar got over her hangover. Mary made it a point to pick up the oranges which fell from the tree, because they are known to ferment when they are on the ground, and she wanted to protect her dog from strong drink.

Weimar liked to ride in the car. She would sit as close to the driver as she could and would help drive. If you started out without her, she would come running and leap through the window. As you can well imagine, this was hard on the person just inside that window, so we usually let her in through the door before we started out. When Mary learned to drive, Weimar learned to drive. We often wondered which one was behind the wheel. They would proceed down the driveway to the road and stop. Mary would look right. Weimar would look right. Mary would look left. Weimar would look left. Then they would proceed.

Animals I Have Hated

Mary and Weimar learned to drive.

Even though Weimar lacked training, I decided to take her out into the hills behind the house to see what she would do with blue quail. She had no trouble making her way through the cactus, as she hunted ahead of me. Inadvertently, she stumbled over a covey of quail. She must have caught them by surprise, because they broke and flew instead of running, as they usually do. The noise scared that good-for-nothing dog. She raced towards me and tried to jump into my lap, which I did not have, because I was trying to make my way through what seemed like a jungle of cactus. I landed in the cactus, holding her. After she settled down, I put her down and then tried to get all of the cactus spines out of me. My thoughts about that dog were not very pleasant. If I had had a gun with me, it would have been a Weimar gun rather than a quail gun. The rest of the afternoon, as we roamed the brush, she stayed behind me rather than in front of me.

Weimar

Several months later, my reasoning power left me again, and I took her out to see if she was any good at running rabbits. They do not make any noise, and they run the other way. She was out in front again, and either she found a rabbit, or it found her. Anyway, she was heading back towards me before the rabbit had a chance to start running. This time I flattened out on the trail so I would not get knocked into another cactus bush. Have you ever tried to get up with a sixty-pound dog sitting on your shoulders which doesn't plan on getting off anytime soon? The only thing I ever found that she would point was rattlesnakes. She was good at that. While I was attending college, I would go out at night with a fellow named Earl and catch rattlesnakes. We shipped them to a snake farm over in Louisiana. Business was good. While I used Weimar a time or two, I was always afraid that a rabbit would chase her towards me while I was handling a snake.

In time Weimer and I came to an agreement. When she got scared, she would not make a flying leap into my lap. At least that's the agreement I thought we had. Periodically I would take her and go out into the hills in the middle of the night and call predators. The call sounded like a rabbit in distress. If there were any feral cats or dogs in the area, they would come. Periodically I would call up coyotes, bobcats, javelina, and badgers. By shining the light just over their heads, their eyes would glow. At the time I could identify most of the animals by the color of the eyes. If I moved, the predator would freeze; and if I did not appear right to him, he would depart with haste or fade back into the brush. On these trips I did not carry a rifle, because I was not interested in shooting the predators, simply seeing if I could call them in close and see them. Sometimes the predators would stop at fifty to seventy-five feet away, and I couldn't get them to come any further; other times I didn't realize they were there until they were about fifteen feet away. As you can well imagine, I picked my place to sit where nothing could sneak up behind me and jump on me. One night during the dark of the moon, I hadn't had much luck after calling for about twenty minutes. Weimer slunk up. She was shaking. She crawled into my lap and buried her head under my right arm. She was terrified. She continued to shake. I quit calling, and I started shining the light to see if I could pick up some eyes, but I did not see any. In time Weimer calmed down. We packed up and headed back home. To this day I don't know what scared Weimer. Previously she had been out when I called up coyotes, bobcats, javelin, and even badgers, and they did not scare her. What scared Weimer? Maybe there was a blue quail or a rabbit running around?

Mary taught Weimar to grab a grass straw that she would hold between her teeth. This was funny, until Papa started to blow his nose one evening. Weimar leaped and grabbed the handkerchief as easily as she grabbed the grass straw. Thereafter, cigarettes, handkerchiefs, and other items near the mouth were not safe.

Weimar was hungry all the time, even though we fed her well. Many were the days she would go to the brick plant and raid the men's lunch pails. In due time they learned to keep their lunches in their cars, with the windows rolled up.

After college, the US government sent me on a Grand Tour. Weimar stayed home and took care of my Pontiac car. Paul, a local farmer, needed a vehicle, so he asked to rent the Pontiac. A deal was made, and he drove off. He parked a mile from the house to check a field on foot. When he returned to the car, Weimar had taken possession and would not let him near the car. Paul walked to the house and told Papa about the dog. They drove back to the Pontiac. Papa introduced Paul to Weimar. After that, Weimar accepted Paul and let him drive the Pontiac, as long as she got to sit beside him. Paul offered to buy the Pontiac if Weimar was thrown in; however, Mary would not sell her dog.

After basic training, I returned to La Puerta. Of course, I was proudly wearing my uniform. As I got out of the car, I got too close to Mary. Weimar protected Mary by tasting my leg. Apparently she recognized the taste. She didn't know whether to be ashamed of herself or joyful at my return.

Weimar

Weimar obtained pleasure from the simple things of life. During the summer, she would catch locusts (cicadas, to you educated folk) and hold them in her mouth. They would buzz. She would get a stupid expression on her face. When locusts were not available, she caught English sparrows off the clothesline "to have and to hold" in her mouth.

When Mary was in high school, she came down with a severe case of strep throat, that is Mary, not Weimar. Weimar found a three-foot rattlesnake in the backyard; so in the best of tradition, she pointed. When her boy didn't come to catch it (I was in the Army), she barked at it. After some discussion from the rattlesnake, it bit the end of her nose. As her nose swelled to the size of a grapefruit, Momma didn't know whether to abandon Mary and take Weimar to the vet (thirty-five miles each way), or to get out the rat poison and put the dog out of its misery. Mary moaned, and Weimar moaned. Mary groaned, and Weimar groaned. Mary would not eat, and Weimar would not eat. After many hours of considering her options, Momma decided she had more time and money invested in Mary, so she stayed with Mary and let Weimar suffer. Over the next day or so, the swelling started dropping. Within a week, she was catching locusts, but she gave up pointing rattlesnakes.

When the family moved to Schertz, Texas, Weimar became a city dog and learned about chain link fences. For several years she could leap over them without a problem, but like all of us, she finally slowed down and let the chain link fence confine her. While she was supposed to be an outside dog, she had other ideas, and learned that when someone was entering the house, she could hit them with her side and knock them out of the way and slip into the house ahead of them. Once inside, she was very difficult to remove.

In time Weimar died from old age. Momma stated that she did not want another dog, since no dog could replace Weimar. Mary and Wayne, Mary's husband, refused to believe her and got her a collie puppy. While I do not know what happened that Christmas day, Mary took the puppy home that afternoon, and it never re-turned to Momma's house. In time a rat terrier joined Momma and was adopted. When it died, a part-Basenji from the animal shelter joined the family. Rosie would sleep on Momma's feet; and when Momma needed to get up during the night, Rosie would go lick Mary in the face to get Mary up to help.

An interesting footnote to the Weimar story is that when I was getting prepared to head to Schertz, Texas, for Papa's funeral, a Weimar-type dog showed up at our house in Castroville. It was a male, rather than a female like Weimar, but it used the same maneuver to get into the house as Weimar had, and it was just as hard to extract from the house.

Pigeons

Pigeons are everywhere that you don't want them to be. I have heard that when the human race is extinct, the world will be populated by cockroaches and pigeons. That may be stretching things, but when you have pigeons where you don't want them, it sure sounds reasonable. At the brick plant we had fine dust, and the question came up whether this fine dust could cause silicosis.

Author's Note: *More recently I have learned that silicosis is usually caused by crystalline silica, and the fine dust that we had at the brick plant was amorphous (or non-crystalline) silica and alumino-silicates. Chances are the fine dust would not have caused silicosis among the workers, but we didn't know that.*

Since there were numerous pigeons that roosted in the rafters at the brick plant and were exposed to the same fine dust that the workers were, I was asked by the plant management to come up with a study to see whether the fine dust was causing any problems in the lungs of the pigeons. Back then we did not have the Internet to help with our research, so I spent many hours in the library paging through many volumes of forgotten lore and ended up writing a proposal. In simplest terms, the proposal required me to capture pigeons, weigh them, determine their overall condition, butcher them, sex them, save the lungs in alcohol, and then examine the lungs under a microscope. Many PhD proposals are not as detailed as this research proposal was.

That was the simple part; the next part required me to climb up into the rafters in the middle of the night and sneak up on the pigeons. This was the dangerous part of the job, and one slip could result in falling twenty-five to thirty feet onto machinery. At least the machinery was not running. I didn't feel any of my crew should be exposed to that danger, so I took on that job myself. After all, when I was a kid crawling around in the mesquite trees, I often had a belt or a rope attached to the back of my pants as a tail. People thought that I must have been at least half monkey. Holding on with one hand and usually at least one foot, I would reach out and grab a pigeon, lock its wings so it could not fly, and drop it to my waiting crew below.

My crew consisted of two junior-level biology students. We went over the purpose of the study and all of the techniques that were going to be used. They assured me that they could do just as good a job as I could, so I should relax and let them do their job. They would examine the pigeon for mites and other external parasites, check the color of the skin, check to see whether the bird was completely feathered, and weigh it. They would record this information; then they would kill the pigeon, butcher it, and process it, so we had pigeon lungs and one leg (for aging) preserved in individual, numbered containers. Those numbers would match the data sheet for that particular bird.

While all of this was going on, I continued to silently crawl around in the rafters and captured about thirty of the thirty-five pigeons that lived there. This took me over two hours. When I got down, I had no intention of ever crawling up there again. Those pigeons that I had not captured moved to a new location, so for a time the brick plant shed was pigeon-free. The workers considered that this was a major success. All of our glass sample containers were carefully packed in cardboard boxes, and we headed home. It was a couple days before I had time to take the sample containers and start examining the lungs with a microscope. When I did, I had a little shock. There was not a single lung in any of the sample bottles. My carefully-trained crew of biology students had saved gizzards. Without any pigeons left at the plant, it was not possible to proceed with the research project.

Pigeons

I learned something with this research project. Well-qualified and well-briefed people can still make errors, and it is the leader's job to ensure that those errors don't happen.

Over the next forty or so years I tried to stay away from pigeons. We had them at a milling facility in Knippa, Texas. The facility was shut down and mothballed. We had a potential buyer, but the potential buyer needed some specific measurements, so I went out and took measurements. Some of the measurements were easy, such as how long the legs on each silo were. I was asked to determine the measurement of the height of the silo, as well as the diameter without the legs attached, and to take measurements of each bag house on top of each silo.

Author's Note: *A bag house is a dust collection system. It contains felt bags that separate the dust from the airstream. To keep the bags from plugging up, the bag house contains a shaker. The most common shaker is a motor attached to an unbalanced wheel. Every fifteen minutes or so, the motor is energized, and the dust is shaken out of the bags. The bag houses were mounted on top of the silos, so that when the bags were shaken, the dust collected could fall into the silo.*

After taking the initial measurements, I was up on top of one of the silos. The top of the silo was one hundred and two feet above the concrete pavement below. The bag house was another twenty or so feet higher. The wind was blowing, and the silo rocked back and forth. This rocking was slight, but it seemed like the silo was moving six to eight inches back and forth. I measured the diameter of the bag house and then climbed up its side, so I could take measurements of its height. All was going well as I reached the top of the ladder and reached across the top of the bag house to grab a piece of steel framing. I grabbed a pigeon. I don't know who was more shocked, me or the pigeon. I could handle grabbing a pigeon, but what scared me was when its companion flew off in a clatter of wings. What do you do when you're one hundred and twenty-two feet up in the air, holding onto a pigeon? After I turned the pigeon

Animals I Have Hated

loose, and after my heart rate returned to about normal, I measured the height of the bag house and then slowly worked my way down to ground level. I moved to the next silo and repeated the process, except that there were no pigeons on top of the second bag house.

College Roommates

While attending college, I lived in a garage apartment owned by one of the biology professors. Rather than pay rent, I did yard work. She had a jaguarundi (a long, dark cat about twice the size of a house cat that is native to South Texas, Mexico, and on into South America) which was her house guest, and periodically she would place it on a long leash outside. With time, I got acquainted with the jaguarundi. She would tolerate me up to about three feet from her. It was only a few months before she died of old age that she would allow me to pet her without disciplining me with her sharp claws.

While living there, I went on several biological field trips to Mexico as the chief-cook-and-bottle-washer. Since Papa did this for the Senator, I wonder if the trait is genetic. On one of those trips, the professor in charge purchased a margay kitten. A margay is a jungle cat that is a little larger than a house cat but is marked like an ocelot. Many people thought it was a young ocelot. Upon our return to Texas, the kitten was installed in my one-room apartment. While she never became tame, she tolerated me.

At Christmas, I received a fruit-and-meat basket from Rio Clay Products where I had a summer job. For the first time in my college career, I was to eat T-bone steak. As the steak cooked, the cat slept on the dresser. When I moved away from the hot plate, the cat jumped across the room, knocked the pie tin off the skillet, grabbed the steak, and leaped back to the dresser. We argued; however, I did not eat T-bone steak that night.

To keep the food bill down, I regularly took a shotgun out and shot grackles. If I couldn't get at least six for a ten-cent shell, I held my fire. Daily I gave the cat three grackles. She would take them to the bathroom to eat them. Once when I picked up the dirty clothes box to head to the washateria, the cat got pugnacious. After escaping from the apartment, I walked to the washateria. Even though it was crowded, I found two washers near each other, so I dumped my dirty clothes on the floor to sort them. As ten grackles rolled out, I understood why the cat was upset. What I couldn't understand was why the two elderly ladies were upset. I hadn't taken **their** food storehouse. After that, I sorted the clothes before I headed off to the washateria. Originally I had planned on using the word Laundromat, but I could not explain to my editor why Laundromat was capitalized and washateria was not.

In time the margay taught itself to use the commode, but I never could teach her to flush it.

On some nights she would sleep across my neck; and if I moved, her growl would tell me that I should keep still. Remember, this was South Texas, and I did not have any air conditioning.

She hated dogs; and if a dog would come to the door, she would head through the screen on the door and take out after it. In time she would return. Dogs learned to stay away from the door to my apartment, and I became quite adept at replacing screen wire.

Evelyn was a very practical older friend. She was two years ahead of me in school and was probably two years older than I was. Her father was a deputy sheriff, and she took it upon herself to keep an eye on me. When she became engaged, rather than opting for an engagement ring, she opted for a window air conditioner for their first apartment when they got married a week after she graduated. When another field trip was scheduled, I arranged for Evelyn to come to my apartment and feed the cat. After we were deep into Mexico, a thought occurred to me. I had not told Evelyn that she should not pet the cat. I had visions of coming home to find blood all over my apartment from the cat shredding Evelyn's delicate hands. Apparently I did not need to be concerned, for when I returned after a week, I found Evelyn sitting in my rocking chair, holding the cat and petting her. She sprayed some of her perfume on one of my good leather gloves and that became the cat's glove. Anytime I attempted to pick up the glove, the cat (not Evelyn) became pugnacious, and I learned that relationships can develop that I never dreamed would be possible.

At one point, when the margay was not living with me, I obtained a screech owl and named it Evelyn, after the friend who gave a perfectly good leather glove to an obnoxious cat. When I next wrote home, I included a paragraph that said, "Evelyn is now living with me."

A close family friend, who was known to gossip, was visiting when the letter arrived, so Momma read it aloud. When she got to the part about Evelyn, she added as if reading, "She is a white mouse that I got from the college. I think she is expecting." Momma always put the best construction on everything.

Pin-Up Photography

When in the military, mail from home is important. In order to receive large quantities, one must write on a regular basis. While in the Army, I wrote the following letter to my mother:

"Dear Momma,

After much thought and many hours of contemplation, I discerned that your comments on my pin-up photography were condoning girl-chasing. Not only were you condoning girl-chasing, but you were actually encouraging it. Please consider the following with regards to such a dangerous subject:

a. Who wants a picture of a girl at thirteen magnifications?

b. Who would encourage the photographer to work out the techniques to get fifty magnifications?

c. How can a person photograph a girl while 'making out' with her?

d. Is it considered appropriate to hang the finished photographs of a cute girl on the bulletin board?

e. Why take the photographs to begin with, if it is not considered appropriate to display them on the bulletin board?

f. Can photographing a girl be as stimulating as crawling on hands and knees in the latrine trying to get a perfect shot of a cockroach?

g. How does one keep the girl model from talking back?

h. How can a photographer remember the various techniques of photography when around a girl?

i. Where can as many suitable girl models be found as we have suitable cockroach models in the barracks?

Your son"

Conditions would have to be very bad to make a person write a letter like that to his mother. Let's look into this story and get the facts behind it.

After joining the Army, I found that I could no longer follow my hobby of photographing good-looking girls in good-looking poses. It took me only six months to discover that one did not find numerous young ladies hanging around the barracks. This disturbed me to no end, so I was forced to look farther afield to find them. Shortly, I discovered that the young ladies I found were not my old girlfriends, so how could I approach them on the subject of girl photography? After three sleepless nights, I approached the fellow in the next bunk and asked for his advice. He said, "Wise up, Punk. You should broaden your interests." Looking back on it, I am sure that he meant I should get acquainted with the girls on their own terms and draw out their interests. At the time, such a wild thought did not occur to me. Here is what happened.

My only interest was the final photo of the teenage female, so I started noticing other "types" of teenage females. There was the young female squirrel in the Sweet Gum Tree by my window; in an Oak Tree across the street there lived a young female starling; here and there I noted several others.

As soon as I had a chance, I set up my camera and tried my hand at this new type of Glamour Photography–Failure.

Not being the type to give up easily, I tried again–Failure.

In a fit of depression I went back to my old love–Human Teenage Female Photography. Since I had not completed the course in "Girl-Charming" that I was taking, I again met failure. Besides the model talking back, I discovered that I could not keep my mind off my model when trying to photograph her. This led to other problems... Several weeks later, after I had decided to give up photography altogether, I saw a new "type" of female teenager. This was the nymph stage of the famous German cockroach. Quickly I got out my camera. My models being very small, I had a few technical problems to work out. After four sessions with my new models, I obtained some excellent results. Quickly I made duplicates of my valuable photos and sent them to the members of my fan club (friends and relatives); then I put a few copies up on the local bulletin boards.

Ain't he cute?

Results came quickly. Although I was completely happy with the results, I discovered that some few members of my fan club were not. I received several letters that were similar to the excerpt below that came from my mother:

"Your photo of the roach may be a wonderful piece of technical know-how, but I must say that your choice of a model leaves me completely cold. I realize that roaches are most certainly more prevalent than pretty girls, but I think you would get a certain amount of fun out of hunting a prettier model, and I firmly believe that if you search diligently, you will find a more photogenic pin-up."

Other letters came in praising my wonderful accomplishments. Several persons even asked for instructions on how to take such breathtaking photographs. While all of these letters were coming in, a series of notes was pinned up under the photos that were on the bulletin boards. One of these notes read, "Pin-up of the Week– 'THE FEMALE'." Another said, "A photo of your pet roach to send home, only three dollars and ninety-eight cents." I believe the notes just quoted tend to indicate a favorable reaction to my photos. After due time, I sat down and answered all of my fan mail. The persons who did not react favorably to my wonderful photographs were mailed letters similar to the one quoted at the first of this article. I revealed my secrets in the following letter to the persons who showed a genuine interest:

"To all interested fans,

Here are a few pointers on entering the fascinating profession of cockroach photography. Be sure to read them carefully; after that, take them with a grain of salt.

a. Get a camera (it is helpful if you want to take photographs).

b. Select your model very carefully (you may mash her if you select her roughly).

c. Get an assistant (he can explain everything to those little men in the white coats).

d. Wear shin guards (some models tend to get excited, and this may cause your assistant to get excited).

e. Practice before you put film in the camera (it's cheaper that way, and anyway, if you are in it for the fun, you may not want the photos).

f. Be careful if you include more than one model in a picture (some censors may consider it pornography).

g. If you intend to sell the pictures, you should get a model release from each identifiable model.

h. If at first you do not get professional-looking results, just remember, what professional would do something like this?

i. If you place your model in the refrigerator for a few minutes before photographing her, she will not run as fast. (If left in over ten minutes, she may get over-weight.)

Animals I Have Hated

j. Set up a sign "Mad Scientist at Work. Do Not Disturb." (Maybe a few kids will believe it.)

k. If anyone asks you what your name is, give him a fictitious name.

If you have any questions after trying this wonderful new sport, do not hesitate to let me know. I may not be able to answer your questions, but maybe we could get a laugh out of them.

John Doe"

I believe that all of you will agree that the points made in both of the letters are very important. After you have tried this new sport, I believe you will become a dedicated photographer of cockroaches.

Author's Note: *The ability to track and photograph cockroaches on the run led to developing a system which I mounted on a rifle stock. It consisted of a bellows-scope (close-up lenses were not available for cameras in that day and time) and flash units that were synchronized so when the subject was in focus, the exposure was perfect. This led to an assignment to photograph mosquitoes in flight. An Army Major was working on a field guide to Vietnamese mosquitoes. With time I got so good that after shooting one hundred shots, one mosquito was in the center of the field and in a position that was acceptable. With thirty-two mosquito species on my list to photograph, I was less than halfway through when the Major's boss determined that one could not see a mosquito in flight well enough to be able to use a photograph to identify it, and that part of the project was canceled.*

The Fish Tank

N ancy, my sister who was three years and two days younger than me, gave me yet another putdown. Easter holidays had arrived, and I caught a bus home from college. The bus had dropped me off beside the highway, and I had walked about three-fourths of a mile to the house carrying everything I needed in a paper grocery sack. A suitcase was not in my budget. Even before I got to the door, she was giving me a tongue-lashing. She, a mere high school student, was all over me. I was not to interfere. I was not to take the credit. I would have agreed, but I did not know what she was talking about. That came out over supper two hours later.

The family was living outside of La Puerta, which is outside of Rio Grande City, Texas. It was on the property of Pozzolana, Inc., and Rio Clay Products, a clay brick plant. This was a dry and dusty part of Texas that averaged twenty to twenty-five inches of rain per year and currently was about fifteen years behind schedule. The hills behind the house were a gray-green color that showed that something was alive, but just barely. Town was five miles away, and the girls did not have many friends since the family had moved into the area the previous summer. Nancy and Mary had asked Papa if they could build a swimming pool. After the initial approval, serious negotiations had started. Papa would have someone use the brick plant dozer to dig the hole. Papa would buy or beg the materials. Nancy and Mary would do all of the block-laying and plastering. Papa would show them how to lay block and plaster. These negotiations had been going on during the previous six weeks, and Nancy did not want me to take any credit for building the swimming pool.

I could lay block as well or better than Nancy would ever be able to learn. I could plaster well enough that I could easily have gotten a job as a plasterer if I had been so inclined. If Nancy would allow it, I could save Papa the time of teaching those silly girls how to lay block and plaster. Nancy would not have it. She would allow me to carry block and mix mortar. That was all. Anything else, and she thought that I would be taking credit for building the swimming pool. What Nancy did not realize was that mixing mortar correctly was half the job of laying block or plastering. Doing it right produced a creamy mix that was a delight to work with. Doing it like most people did, produced a harsh mix that was hard to work with.

Author's Note: *While Herb's skills were not at that level yet, eventually he became a leading expert on mortars and plasters, and has regularly been referred to as the world's leading expert on stucco.*

From Easter on through the middle of the summer, the girls worked. I knew that they were going to quit because the job was too big—thirty feet long and fourteen feet wide, by six feet deep at the deep end. When college let out for the summer, I came home to work in the brick plant and figured I would be begged to lay block. It never happened. I could mix mortar and carry block, but I was not allowed to lay any block.

By early August, the pool was complete, and we started filling it. The pool held water and did not have any cracks. There is no way that two silly girls could have done that job, but they did. The pool did not have any cracks until the next year when a sand filter was added, but that is a different story.

The pool was popular every day in August after it was filled. September brought school, so the pool was used for late afternoon swims and for weekend swims. By late October the weather had started to cool off, and some late afternoon swims were missed.

The Fish Tank

Thanksgiving saw an end to the year's swimming. In south Texas, what do you do with a swimming pool that is too cold to swim in?

Nancy will never notice.

Christmas break brought me home with enough time for Papa and me to go fishing at Falcon Lake. We went up for a day trip to El Tigre Island. We packed coffee and everything else we needed, but forgot the coffeepot and coffee mugs. A norther blew in, so we hauled out for lunch and tried to fix coffee to go with the sandwiches. Two rusty tin cans served as our coffeepot and coffee mugs. As cold as we were, it was some of the best coffee we had ever had. Over lunch, while protected with our foul weather gear, six-foot-by-six-foot pieces of black polyethylene plastic, we discussed whether we wanted to head in or not. We had seven large-mouth black bass in the live box. We could clean and ice them down, turn them loose, or try to catch a few more. We decided that we would take the bass home and place them in the swimming pool so we would not have to clean them immediately. Since

Animals I Have Hated

Thanksgiving, Nancy had not been adding chlorine to the pool, and it showed signs of algae growth.

That decided, we put the plug in the bottom of the live box, loaded the boat, and headed for home. After about twenty miles, the heater had warmed us to the extent that we started to talk about how we would explain the bass to the girls. Over the next thirty miles we came to no conclusions, so when we arrived home, we backed the boat under the boat shed, and I caught the bass in the live well and placed them in the pool. We went into the house. Momma wanted to know if we had brought fish for supper, and Papa explained that we had not. Nothing was said about bass in the swimming pool.

After Christmas I went out to re-catch the bass and clean them. Nancy met me by the pool and informed me that I would leave her bass alone. A week later I headed back to college. At Easter the bass were doing well. When I got home in late May, the bass were gone, and the girls and all of their friends were swimming. The bass were not mentioned. The next fall we did not attempt to restock the fish tank. From all of this I learned that no matter how much of an expert one is, at home you are just a good-for-nothing sibling.

White Bass

L et me tell you about white bass fishing at Falcon Lake. Falcon Lake was filled in 1954. Prior to that, there were white bass in the Rio Grande River, but the population was not very great. White bass are not native to the Rio Grande River. They come from East Texas and parts further east, so someone must have stocked the Rio Grande River with white bass. With the filling of Falcon Lake, the population of white bass exploded. The Texas Game, Fish, and Oyster Commission may have helped the explosion by stocking fingerling white bass.

Some white bass fishermen followed the spawning runs in the early spring to the upper reaches of Falcon Lake, but most of us fished for white bass during the summer. White bass school and feed on shad close to the surface. We could spot the schooling white bass and shad by watching for seagulls. When we saw gulls circling and diving, we would know that there was probably a school of white bass underneath that was feeding on shad.

Our normal method of fishing was to troll. We usually used a fourteen-foot V-bottomed aluminum boat with two motors on the back – a Five Hp Johnson for trolling and a Ten Hp Mercury for traveling. We would use a line spreader and spinner that we referred to as Texas Trailers. Even though there was a commercially-available Texas Trailer, and that is where the name came from, we made our own. In fact, we made so many, we sold some to cover the cost of those that we used. On one leg of the line spreader we would attach a diving lure. The most common lure we've used was called a Bomber. It was a wooden lure with a dive plate in front. It would float on the surface until it was moved through the water, at which time it would dive. The depth of the dive was determined by the speed of the boat and the length of line that was let out from the reel. Needless to say, when we would start trolling, one would use short line and another would use a longer line, so that we could be fishing at two different depths. On the other leg of the line spreader, we would attach a spinner. We also fabricated our own spinners and sold enough to cover the cost of those we used.

Normally, within a white bass school, the small fish would be closer to the surface and the larger fish would be further down. "Further down" is a relative term, since it might mean three feet, or it might mean ten feet. Our goal was to catch the larger fish. Normally, the white bass would strike the spinner. But it was not unheard of on any given trip to catch several sets of doubles. A double did not fight as much as a single, because the two fish would be fighting against each other rather than fighting against the fisherman.

After we had located a school of white bass and if they tended to be stationary, we would stow our Texas trainers and would cast spinners into the school. This had a good side and a bad side. The bad side was that the spinners had to pass through the small white bass before they could get to the large white bass that we were after. The good side was that we almost always had a fish on, if the school remained stationary, even if only two of us were casting from the boat. To increase our chances of catching the larger white bass, we often attached a split-shot sinker or two, about two or three feet in front of the spinner. This would allow the spinner to sink at a rapid rate and hopefully get the spinner out of the reach of the little fish before one of them grabbed it.

After catching a few white bass each (I remember a limit of fifty white bass per day, and then the Texas Game, Fish, and Oyster Commission lowered the limit to twenty-five per day), we would regularly use a pair of pliers to remove the barbs from the hooks.

White Bass

Six more fish for Herb to clean.

This served several purposes:
- It allowed us to unhook the fish easier,
- It gave the fish a sporting chance; actually that sporting chance was not very much because as long as one kept a little tension on the line, the hooks would not come unhooked,
- It allowed us to unhook each other easier, since we were fishing in close quarters, and
- We could turn loose the little fish and hope to replace them with larger fish.

It got downright tiresome to limit-out with white bass in as little as forty-five minutes. When there were four of us in the boat (my two sisters, Papa, and me), you know who got to clean those two hundred fish, or later those one hundred fish. I cannot recall any time that either of my sisters cleaned a fish. One problem with cleaning white bass that you do not have with black bass is that they have a couple dorsal spines that are much sharper and stiffer than those on black bass. This means that with each fish that you clean, you get at least one puncture wound. With one hundred white bass, that makes one hundred or more puncture wounds. With two hundred white bass, that makes at least two hundred puncture wounds. After the second or third day of fishing, I was ready to go home and go back to work. There were times I thanked the Texas Game, Fish, and Oyster Commission for lowering the limit. Fishing should be fun, but it can be a lot of work.

White Bass

Gar

There were fish in Falcon Lake besides white bass. Of course, the largemouth black bass was considered the king of the lake. As I would wade along the shores of El Tigre Island in pursuit of the black bass, I would often see a longnose gar about three-and-a-half feet long. I remember it as being closer to four feet long, but most would tend to think that I was stretching things if I made it that long. In that mile-and-a-half of shoreline that I regularly fished, I did not see more than one gar at a time, and the gar was always about the same size.

Periodically, one of them would make a pass at my lure. Sometimes the pass would result in the jaws of the gar smashing down on the lure. This usually smashed the treble hooks. It also had a tendency to scrape the paint off the wood or worse. With fishing slow, because the gar had chased off all of the bass, I used this as an excuse for not catching anything; I would fish for gar. Casting near a gar and dragging the lure in front of him would usually result in a CHOMP. Gars do not bite or strike; they open their mouths and chomp down on their prey, usually using the side of their mouths, close to the hinge of the jaw so they can exert more force. The gar's mouth is too tough for a hook to penetrate, so the only connection to the gar was his holding the lure in his mighty jaws. As long as I kept tension on the line, the gar would continue to hold on. In this manner I often fought a gar for fifteen to twenty minutes before he would get tired of the game, or he would get too close to me and let go of the hook. To conserve a fishery, many fishermen use a technique called "catch and release." This was catch and auto-release.

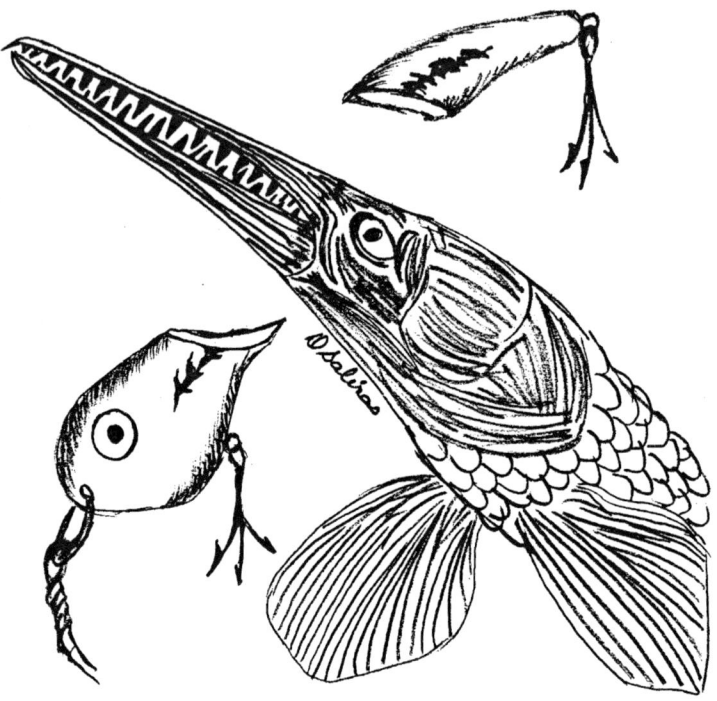

That lure cost me $2.98!

I told Papa about seeing one gar at a time along the one-and-a-half-mile shoreline of El Tigre Island. I then mentioned that I regularly fished for the gar. With a straight face he assured me that it was always the same gar. The gar just followed me around to keep me from catching black bass and to keep me from bothering the other longnose gar in Falcon Lake. I laughed at his concept, but then I started watching and concluded that Papa might be right after all.

There were other gar in the lake. We regularly trot-lined for catfish using live perch or cut bait. These trot-lines would periodically pick up longnose gar. Most of them were in the two-and-a-half-foot to three-and-a-half-foot range. So I knew there were other gar in the lake. In due time I got sick and tired of losing perfectly good Bombers to my friend the gar, so I got a block of wood and tied it onto my fishing line. The gar was as content grabbing the block of wood as he was smashing my expensive Bomber lures. Obviously he knew that the block of wood was not food. I think he was having as much fun as I was having.

In time, I moved away from the area and quit going to Falcon Lake. I wonder, after I quit playing with the gar, whom did he find to play with? That gar taught me that one did not have to land, or even hook, a fish in order to have a good fishing trip.

After I took up kayaking, I often fished on the Medina River within a couple of miles of my home. While using a fly rod, I saw some longnose gar, so I threw a fly at them. A three-foot gar took the fly, held on for a while, and towed the kayak for about one hundred feet. It then turned loose of the fly and went on his way. I started experimenting and found that white streamer flies worked better than the other flies that I tried. Often I would get a tow of up to a quarter of a mile before the gar would choose to release me and let me go on my way. I think they were having as good a time as I was having. I guess they considered this a catch-and-release sport, since they always released me unharmed.

Amchitka Island

D aily I checked my feet to see if webs were growing between my toes. Upon leaving the military, I went to Amchitka Island, Alaska. While on Amchitka Island, I saw lots of rain. As many of you know, Amchitka was a nuclear test site. We won't go into why I was on Amchitka, the type of security clearance I had to have to land on Amchitka, the censorship of all of the mail I wrote, or the work I did while on Amchitka, but we will discuss fishing.

Amchitka Island is about four miles wide and forty-two miles long. It sits between the Bering Sea and the North Pacific Ocean in the quirk in the International Date Line. Except for a couple of islands west of it, it is the closest place in the United States to tomorrow. The weather is maritime—fog or rain about ninety percent of the time during the summer, with highs up to 57 degrees Fahrenheit. Rain is never hard, but a drizzle is so common that one begins to look for mold on the end of one's nose. The island is covered with tundra, and over three hundred fresh-water streams exit the island. In many areas the tundra grows over the stream bank, and what looks like a foot-wide stream may be six feet wide a few feet down.

The fresh waters of the island contain Dolly Varden Char (trout to those who do not know what a char is), stickleback, and a small sculpin. Four species of salmon enter the fresh water to spawn. Each summer, and summer is a relative term, the Dolly Varden Char migrate from fresh water to salt water. The migration is triggered by increasing temperature (also a relative term) and also by increasing water flow. As a result, prior to the migration, Dolly

Varden will congregate near the outlets to the island's streams and lakes. After spending forty-five to ninety days in salt water, the Dolly Varden return to fresh water to over-winter. During that brief stay in salt water, they usually more than double in weight.

One of the lakes, Silver Salmon Lake, is a graben. That's a fancy word for a lake that is formed when the land between two faults drops. The sides of the lake where the faults occur tend to be vertical, and such lakes are often deep. Silver Salmon Lake, while only a hundred yards wide, was loaded with Dolly Varden. Using both a spinning rig and a fly rod, I fished near the outlet of the lake. Even though I could see the fish, and I knew they were hungry because they had not eaten all winter, they would not strike my lures. Dr. Helms fished beside me and regularly got strikes and landed fish. He showed me a few tricks about retrieving, and suddenly I was getting strikes.

One day, while fishing there with my friend, Kenneth Anton, a welder, I had tremendous luck. Before we talk about that tremendous luck, let me tell you a little about Ken. Ken was a storyteller. He could spin the wildest yarns in a manner that made them believable. He had his own ideas about fishing. His rig consisted of a bait casting rod with an underhanded spinning reel mounted on it. For line he had heavy braided line that one would use on a surf-type bait casting reel. At the end of the line he had a snap swivel. It was fairly large, so he could operate it easily with his work-enlarged fingers. Attached to the snap swivel was a dry fly. If he dropped the fly on the water, the snap swivel would carry it to the bottom at a rapid rate. He held the bait casting rod in a normal position for use. The underhanded spinning reel was over the rod. While fishing, he would remove about as much line as it took to position the fly at the butt of the rod. He would sneak up to the shore, dangle the fly in the water, or maybe I should say on the water, and say "Here fishy, Here fishy." As surprising as it may seem, he caught fish. He caught many more fish than I caught, before I received instructions from Dr. Helms; and afterwards, we were usually neck-to-neck in our ability to catch fish.

That day I was using a fly rod. In 1968 fly rods were not as sophisticated as they are now, or maybe I should rephrase that statement. Fly rods I could afford were not as sophisticated as fly rods that I can currently afford. What I had was a fiberglass rod approximately eight feet long. The fly line was a level fly line that had to be waxed each time after it'd been used; otherwise the fly line would sink. On that particular day, in twenty-nine casts, and what I refer to as a cast was getting the line and the fly out in front of me and on the water, I had tremendous luck. If I made a cast without hooking the back of my neck, tundra, or anything else, that was a plus. In those twenty-nine casts, I had char rise and strike at the fly twenty-eight times. Of those twenty-eight strikes, I hooked twenty-five char. Most of those twenty-five char were landed. They ranged in length from about fourteen inches to about thirty inches. This being the end of their winter dormant period, they were thin, very thin. If I had not known better, I would have thought some of them were snakes, they were so thin. Since there was no meat on these char, they were released.

Two days later, on July 3, we received a rainfall that caused the outfall creek from Silver Salmon Lake to rise about four inches. In a matter of a few hours, I don't think there was a char left in Silver Salmon Lake. However, fishing in the Bering Sea a few hundred feet offshore was wonderful. Each day the char seemed to be a little heavier, and a little fatter, than the day before.

It was not until August 27 that char started returning to the lake. They came in with rising water levels. While we often think of fish swimming right-side-up, the water in some areas was so low that the fish swam on their sides. What a strange life. Lying dormant or near dormant in a freshwater stream under overhanging tundra for ten months of the year and then having less than two months of feasting. Apparently they understood that when there was an opportunity, they should grasp the opportunity. I filed this information away and used it on numerous occasions over the years to grasp opportunities when they showed themselves.

As the Dolly Varden migrated into fresh water, salmon also came into fresh water to spawn. More than once, several of us would straddle a creek and pick up salmon as they swam or flopped between our feet. Since man was the only predator on the island, and there were only a few of us, our fishing efforts "a la bear" did not have much impact on the migration of the salmon.

Mary

I thought about naming this chapter, "Mary, Mary, Quite Contrary," but it was too long for one line. Sometimes it does not pay to get up in the morning. I had a few days off from a troubleshooting job and was visiting my parents. My brother-in-law, Wayne, was working at the fire station where he was twenty-four-hours-on and forty-eight-hours-off. My sister, Mary, asked me to take her fishing. I should have known better, but apparently I didn't. We loaded my car and headed to Lake Dunlap, about fifteen miles away.

Wayne's mother had a cabin on Lake Dunlap. We remembered the key to the cabin and the key to the lock that chained the Jon boat to a tree. Fishing tackle was in the cabin. I pulled out the spade and dug a few earthworms, then launched the boat and attached the motor. With Mary in the boat, the motor coughed a time or two and then decided to run. We headed down the lake for a few hundred yards to a place where a tree overhung the lake and bluegill sunfish were known to hang out.

Mary liked to fish with a cane pole, so I joined her with a cane pole rather than with the spinning rod and reel that I preferred. Being a college graduate and a schoolteacher, Mary had a few strange ideas. She did not think it was fitting for such a sophisticated young lady to have to bait a hook with an earthworm. I baited her hook. As time passed and I caught undersized bluegill and turned them loose, she kept taking the worms away from the fish, and in the process she would lose the worm. She did not seem to be able to comprehend that you needed to leave the worm, with hook in it, down with the fish until the fish ate the worm. In yanking her line out of the water, she caught tree branches. Since sophisticated young ladies do not climb trees, I got to do the retrieval. In time, with all she was doing wrong, she hooked a bluegill that was all of seven inches long. As she yanked it out of the water and swung it towards me, she screamed, "Herbie, do something." As I looked up, the bluegill hit me in the face and the first spiny ray of the dorsal fin imbedded itself in my nose. As the fish flopped, it would have put out my eyes if I had not been wearing sunglasses. To this day, I carry a reminder of that fishing trip in the form of a scar on my nose. Every time I look into a mirror, I remember my little sister.

That day, I learned two lessons. One, never take a woman fishing who is not your wife, and two, never fish with a woman who cannot bait her own hooks.

The world-famous Texas Singing Quail

The next time I gave in to Mary's request that I take her fishing was fifteen years later. Wayne was hosting a fishing tournament on Choke Canyon Reservoir for his clients. Mary and I ran the camp. My wife had sense enough to stay home. Several of the clients from Wisconsin treated us like their personal servants and made life hectic. But they were clients, and the client is always right. When one of these Wisconsinites pointed out a meadowlark and demanded to know what it was, I assured him that it was a Texas Singing Quail. This led to more questions, and more answers, which I made up on the spot. Later he shared his new-found knowledge with some of the locals who knew better. But back to taking Mary fishing. I did not own a fishing license. When the last dish was washed, and the last demanding client was taken care of, I took her fishing, but carefully left all poles and hooks on the shore. We were a mile from the dock when she discovered that we had forgotten the fishing gear. Instead of going back and getting the fishing gear, we spent our time watching birds. Now *that* was a fun fishing trip, and I did not have a dorsal spine of a fish imbedded in my nose that time. Some of the best fishing trips do not require fishing poles.

In time, I took up kayak fishing. I had attended a seminar concerning fishing in the coastal flats. The second day of the seminar we went out in kayaks. Within a month I had my own kayak. The first time I took my kayak down to the coast to fish among the mangroves, I limited out in redfish in about fifteen minutes. Sitting sidesaddle in my kayak, with my feet dragging the muddy bottom, I had redfish swim up to within touching distance. Obviously I was an expert fisherman and started wondering whether I should set up a kayak guiding service to take people out to catch fish. The next time I took my kayak down to the coast I didn't catch anything; I did not get even a single strike. While that was disheartening, I was glad that it did not occur when I was taking my first paying fishing customer out. To ensure that I could still catch fish, I took another trip to the coast and again I did not catch a single fish. I didn't even have a strike. The next time I was at the coast I was with a friend, and we hired a guide who was the first kayak fishing guide on the Texas coast. His name is Dean Thomas. While my friend got several strikes, and landed one small redfish, I did not get a single strike. At that point I decided it would be better if I kept my day job. Is it any wonder that when I set up my guiding service, I became a nature kayak guide rather than a fishing kayak guide? I did not have to worry about whether I would catch fish. All I had to worry about was ensuring that my clients had a delightful and safe time. I've tried to get Mary into a kayak, but she always has some excuse to not come. The real reason may be that she does not want to go kayaking with me since I have learned to not let her hold a fishing pole when I am close enough to be hooked by her. Back when I was trying to get up enough nerve to ask a young lady out, Momma told me that if I asked a young lady out three times and she turned me down three times without suggesting an alternative, she probably did not want to go out with me. I wonder, does my pesky kid sister not want to go kayaking with me?

Lonesome Polecat

E arly in October of 1973, I moved to Austin, Texas, and took a job with the State. I found an apartment in a large complex. My apartment was on the ground floor, and it overlooked a creek. Woodlands were within five feet of my front door.

Being in a strange town, I felt a few twinges of loneliness. When a large black cat with a pure white triangular marking on its chest ambled in through my open door one evening while I was washing dishes, I decided to make friends. I am not a glutton, but I seldom leave any food when I sit down to eat. A quick survey showed that the cat would have to be satisfied with a piece of bread. She turned up her nose at the offering, and hopped up on my chair and gave me the evil eye. As I finished the dishes and was drying my hands, I decided to pet that cat. She must have had other ideas; for as I approached, she bounced off the chair, hit the floor, bounced up onto the sofa, and landed on the window ledge. Maybe, I decided, I won't pet that cat. She sat there for about an hour, looking at me as if I were trying to starve her. I could not relax with her giving me the evil eye, but she was company. I'm told, but do not believe, that bad company is better than no company at all. As quietly as she came, she went away.

Two nights later, she came back while I was eating Mexican food that I had fixed. Since I make the best tortillas this side of Sixth Street, I took pride in offering to share my bounty with her. She turned it down. Who did she think she was? My feelings were hurt so much that I did not offer her an enchilada or a spoon of frijoles refritos. Quietly she took her place on the windowsill and laid down on a ripening Japanese Persimmon. Why she did not get a backache I'll never know. I got one just watching her. Again, she gave me the evil eye for an hour. As quietly as before, she departed.

Two nights after that, I was eating catfish. Rather than fry catfish, I like to bake them with a little bay leaf, salt, and pepper. I've been called a heretic a few times when I admitted to others how I fixed catfish. After I took the fish out of the oven, I removed most of the meat from the bones and set the bones down on the floor on a piece of tinfoil. As I sat down to eat, the cat slowly approached the bones (and a little meat) and sniffed. The hair on her neck stood on end, and her back arched. Her tail looked like the tail of a scared cat in a cartoon. It must have been a full three inches in diameter. With a hiss and several spits, she hit the fish bones with a left paw and sent them flying across the room. I thought she was going to turn herself inside out, trying to turn around and get out the door. As she flew across the room, she yowled like she had had her tail cut off behind her ears. Two days later, I was down in San Antonio visiting my parents, so was not around to see if she came back. During the following week, I did not see her, so I concluded that she just did not like to be around a heretic.

On Saturday night I cooked short ribs and had some scraps left over, so I put them just outside the door at about 10:30 PM, in case the cat happened to be in the neighborhood and wanted to eat short ribs. Obviously she was not. Another neighborhood cat sampled them. Later the scraps just sat there. About 11:30 PM I looked up from my reading. There was a bushy tail sticking in the door. Since I did not recognize it as belonging to any of the neighborhood cats or dogs, I got up to have a better look. It was a skunk. I sat down and lit up my pipe, the better for him to smell me, and made various movements so that he could hear me. The little fellow was just under four inches high at the shoulder, and did not seem to mind the company. I kept letting him know that he was not alone. Finally he got the bones picked clean. He turned around and walked into the apartment.

Animals I Have Hated

Nice kitty, why don't you go home?

As he looked me over, I talked to him, but made no attempt to get up and shoo him out. After a while (it seemed like ten or twelve hours), he turned and walked under the couch. There was plenty of room under the couch for a big dog, but the coffee table was sitting in a position so that I could not see under the couch. As I sat there looking at first one end of the couch and then the other end, I wondered if I should get up and leave. I guess that I was just too chicken to get up, so I continued to sit there and talk to my new-found friend, "Kitty, don't you know that cats of your stripe are supposed to stay outside? Don't you want to go outside? If you go quietly, I'll put an apple out tomorrow night." I guess the "kitty" had gone to sleep under the couch. I still did not feel brave enough to get up and find out, so I sat there and talked first to it and then to myself. Basically, I called myself every name in the book for leaving the door open, and then asked myself what I would do if he decided to take up residence in my abode. I asked myself what my associates would say at the office if I scared my newfound friend.

Lonesome Polecat

None of my answers to these questions were entirely satisfactory. I mentioned my bribe of an apple again. I was so sleepy by this time that I was repeating myself quite often. I knew that if I stopped, I would fall asleep. Snores might disturb the woods kitty. Additionally, if I angered my friend, I wanted to be awake so I could turn my face. Just as I said the word apple for the fifth time, the skunk came out from under the couch, looked me over again, and then trotted between the coffee table and the couch (all I could see was the big bushy tail) to the door. At the door, he stopped and looked back at me, then headed down the slope toward the creek. I got up, walked to the door, and slowly closed it. Through the window, I watched him until he disappeared.

The next night, I cut an apple into quarters and placed them outside my door. A promise is a promise. I pondered: should I leave the door open for fresh air and for a chance of seeing my new friend? Or should I close it for self-protection? I debated this for about half an hour. All the while, the door remained open.

Could it be that I was so lonesome that if I couldn't make friends with the neighborhood cats, I would make friends with the neighborhood skunks? I wondered what the next tenant would say the first time he left the door open of an evening. I got up and walked to the door. The polecat was busy eating his apple, so I said, "Good night, Kitty." Then I slowly closed the door.

A Funny-Looking Bug

Sometimes I wonder if it's worth getting up of a morning. We all have those days; it's just nice when we don't have two of them in a week, or two of them in a row. Bob Farley got me involved as an adult leader with a Boy Scout Troop. I was not a Boy Scout as I was growing up; and when I would be asked to help out after I grew up, I would always express willingness, but when the scout leader would find that I had not been a Boy Scout, he would point out that I did not meet the qualifications. As the years passed, I developed other interests and was not interested in working with the Boy Scouts. Bob asked me if I would like to serve as an assistant scout leader. I responded, "I would love to, but I was not a Boy Scout as a kid." He responded that that did not matter because the Boy Scouts had a new program just for adult leaders who had not been Boy Scouts. I was trapped.

Bob and I had a group of Boy Scouts out on a camping trip. They tended to run us ragged during the day, but we finally convinced them to set up their tents, fix supper, and eat supper. Since Bob and I were more efficient at doing these chores, we regularly had Scouts coming over wanting to know if they could eat some of our food, especially the Dutch oven cobbler we had made. Each time, we assured them that they needed to set up their own tents, to fix their own supper, to eat their own supper, and to wash their own dirty dishes. After they had finally accomplished this, we started herding them towards their tents. Getting them in their tents was not real difficult. The problem was getting them to turn out their flashlights and quit talking. After things had settled down to some extent, Bob and I headed to our tents. As we did, we saw periodic lights in tents, and we heard comments from the various boys. No matter how much we tried to enforce lights-out and quiet time, there was always something going on. On this particular night as I was drifting off to sleep, one of the younger Scouts said to his companion, "Look at this funny bug." After a moment, "It looks kinda like a crawdad that's been stepped on." That identified it for me as a scorpion. Immediately the other Scout said, "Let's catch it."

Let's catch him.

There was not time to stop them from catching that scorpion. Knowing how painful scorpion stings are, I knew that neither Bob nor I would get any sleep that night. Bob would probably have to drive the Scout in for medical care and then take him home and explain to his parents how he got bit by a scorpion on a supervised Scout camping trip. Not that the medical care would help, but that is what the parents would expect us to do. Bob might make it back to camp by 5:00 am, in time to put on the coffee. I would probably stay in camp with the rest of the troop and be asked a thousand times, "Do you think he is OK?" Or another version of the same question, "Do you think he will live?" No matter how many times I answered that question, it would keep coming because each Scout would be worried. Asking the question would give the Scout a little assurance that everything was OK. It was also one way to not concentrate on the worry. I guess the Lord intervened that evening, because the scorpion escaped. We got all of the Scouts up and discussed scorpions and other creatures of the night, and it was another three hours before we got the Scouts back in their tents and quiet. I think I was leading Scout camping trips because I had been told they were fun. If this was fun, I would hate to do something that was not fun.

Vicious Dogs

W hile working in Arizona, on a regular basis I had dealings with small-time gold miners. On this particular day
I needed to talk to an interesting character. Previously
he held a responsible job with the Valley National Bank in Phoenix,
but when the gold bug bit him, he gave it up and moved to a placer
claim a few miles out of Rye, Arizona. He lived in an old decrepit
travel trailer with his wife or his girlfriend. I never was interested
enough to find out which. On the same claim, his partner had an
even more decrepit travel trailer. For whatever reason, the live-in
companion moved out and moved in with his partner, and the
three continued to work together.

I always worried when going to these small gold mines, because the gold miners tended to be so suspicious of anyone who
came onto "their property." That is, as they defined "their property." It was all National Forest Land, and they had simply staked
claims to mine minerals from the land. Guns were usually in
evidence. I drove up to the mine and parked my pickup in an area
where it could easily be seen from each of the travel trailers, and
from the area where the placer mining was supposedly taking
place. Following good gold-mining etiquette, I honked and remained in my pickup for about five minutes. Then I honked again
and got out of my pickup and stood beside it. There is no way I was
going to walk up to one of the trailers, or to the placer mining area.
People had gotten shot doing that sort of thing. After waiting for
another three or four minutes, I was thinking about getting in my
pickup and departing, when the door of one of the travel trailers
opened, a Doberman came out, and someone hollered, "Gittem." I

couldn't make it back into my pickup before the dog was on me, so I stood perfectly still. The Doberman came to a screeching halt at my feet, reached out, and licked my hand. Then the mine owner came out with a big grin on his face and said, "Scared you, didn't it?" Needless to say, I was not particularly anxious to talk business with this gentleman, and concluded that anyone who would train a dog in that manner was very short on intelligence. Since then, I have not changed my mind.

On most days, I forget that I have an advanced degree in aquatic ecology, because I have seldom used it during my professional life. Maybe my love for kayaking with nature is a holdover from that period in my life. At one point I was researching Macrobrachium. These are a genus of freshwater prawn. I was interested in determining whether I could raise some of the native species in captivity. An Indonesian species had been successfully raised in captivity. For most people, these would be considered freshwater shrimp, but there is a very clear distinction between prawn and shrimp. At the moment, I have no idea what that distinction is, but back then it was important to me. The largest are nearly a yard long, while other species are only a few inches long. Some, but not all of them, migrate to brackish water to mate and lay eggs. They then work their way upstream. At some point in their life cycle, the young prawn head upstream.

To get some of the references I needed, I went to the San Marcos University Library. That's not the real name of the library, but the name of the university seems to change whenever the Texas Legislature is in session, so I never can keep up with what it is currently called. Before all of the name-changing started, it was Texas State Teachers' College, and its claim to fame was that Lyndon Johnson went to school there to get his teaching certificate. I went in, spent several hours, and was ready to leave. A security guard stopped me before I exited the front door. There was a Doberman just outside the door not letting anyone enter or depart. The security guard stated they were trying to find the owner, so that the owner could remove the dog without harm to either the dog or to people. Within about fifteen minutes a gentleman arrived whom the dog recognized. The gentleman attached a leash to the dog's collar, and they departed. I wonder what would have happened if I had gone outside. Would the Doberman have licked my hand like the Doberman at the gold mine? I'm glad I did not have the opportunity to test the Doberman. Frankly, I do not like aggressive dogs, whether they are big enough to do some real damage or whether they are just yap-yap dogs. Dog owners have a responsibility, but many ignore it.

Several years ago I had some discussions with a gentleman who very aggressively claimed that pit bulls were very gentle and would never hurt anyone. If anyone disagreed with him, he would get fighting mad. He named one of his dogs Lucifer and the other Satan, and could not see why I though such names might subconsciously give the dogs a message that they should be evil. We never had a conversation when we did not disagree.

I kept having to remind myself that my mother always told me that people are people, and they cannot help their idiosyncrasies. No matter how many times I told myself that, it just did not sink in, so I remembered how she could distance herself emotionally from people who were not on her favorites list.

The Quail Farm

B ack when I was a kid, I raised chickens. While sometimes I would buy day-old chicks at the feed store, on other occasions I would set eggs under a broody hen and hatch out my own chicks. I tried raising quail but was not successful.

Author's Note: A hen whose instinct for motherhood has not been bred out of her (White Leghorns and other high-egg-laying breeds) sometimes goes broody. This occurs after she has laid a clutch (a group) of ten or a dozen eggs. Her temperature goes up a little bit; she becomes protective of her eggs; she stays on her nest and keeps them warm. For brief periods each day, she will get off the nest to eat and drink, but then head back to the nest. After twenty-one days, if the eggs are fertile, they hatch, and the hen starts taking care of her brood.

When we were living in Knippa, I decided to try it again. My friend, Lloyd, borrowed his aunt's tabletop incubator with an automatic turning mechanism. I ordered Japanese quail eggs, probably twenty-five of them, but I don't remember for sure. In time some of them hatched and grew to adulthood.

The reason I was interested in raising the Japanese quail rather than bobwhite quail is the literature said that the Japanese quail, which have been raised in captivity in Japan for many centuries, would start laying eggs when they were as young as seven weeks old and that they would lay about three hundred eggs per year. A bobwhite quail needed to be nearly a year old before it started laying eggs, and then it would lay only a few dozen eggs each year. So about two months after the first quail chicks hatched, I was starting to get eggs from my quail. I set some of them, and they hatched. This was a lot of fun, and Lloyd and I each butchered some quail for eating, and we each tried pickling some quail eggs. When I tried cooking quail eggs sunny-side-up in a skillet for breakfast, I got tired breaking the eggs because it took so many, and I ended up adding shells to my breakfast.

That is when an error in judgment occurred. I saw an advertisement for a Georgia Quail Farm incubator and a Georgia Quail Farm hatcher in the San Antonio newspaper. The incubator would hold twelve hundred quail eggs. I could buy both of them for three hundred dollars. I would never want to set twelve hundred quail eggs, but I did not have to fill the units up. Sooner or later I was going to have to return the tabletop incubator, and to replace it would have cost close to two hundred dollars. It seemed that this was a good investment. It would allow me to raise more quail and set the eggs whenever I needed to set them.

I drove into San Antonio and purchased the incubator and the hatcher. Then I scrubbed them and disinfected them. No sense in introducing someone else's diseases into my operation. With the units set up and turned on, I started monitoring the temperature and humidity. After a couple days, the temperature and humidity were right where I wanted them. A schedule soon developed with setting eggs very early on Thursday of each week. Since the eggs hatched in sixteen days, I would remove them from the incubator, which had an automatic turning mechanism, on day fifteen, which was a Friday, and place those eggs in the hatcher. The hatcher had trays that were level and did not turn. Late Friday night the eggs would start hatching, and on Saturday morning the eggs would have hatched and the chicks would have dried out. The baby quail were about the size of the marbles I played with as a kid. I would remove the chicks and place them in a brooder pen.

Since I had the ability to hatch more eggs, suddenly I had the desire to set more eggs. Even though I had never intended to fill that incubator up, soon I was hatching about three hundred and fifty quail chicks every Saturday morning. I made arrangements so

Animals I Have Hated

that Lloyd would take the hatch one Saturday morning, and then Mr. Niemeyer, who owned the town of Cockaburra Flats, would take the hatch the next Saturday morning. Getting off the subject for a moment, the museum at Cockaburra Flats was full of many strange and interesting things. For example, there was a hatchet that was one hundred and eighty-seven years old. The wooden handle had been replaced five times, and the metal head had been replaced twice. Now, back to the story. I kept the hatch from the third Saturday morning. This gave us all plenty of quail to raise, to butcher, and to either eat or sell. This was a very nice, fun, money-making hobby. I was proud of myself for putting it together. As most people know, pride comes before a fall.

I just cannot eat another quail.

The first quail cages I built were from wood and hardware cloth. With time, the design of the cages evolved. Build the cages too large, and it was difficult to catch the quail. Build them too small, and there was more time spent feeding and watering them.

The Quail Farm

For my laying cages there was a slight slope to the floor so that the eggs would roll close to the door and I could easily collect them.

One winter it snowed in Knippa. Not just a light dusting which we expected to see every few years, but a foot of snow. The supports for the cages were not designed to handle this load and several cages failed. There were quail all over the place. The cats feasted, and then they quit eating quail. They had had enough. One morning I went out to the shed to start my morning chores. One of the tomcats was sound asleep with two quail sitting on his back, also sound asleep. Even though we did not expect another snow like we had, this gave me the motivation to switch to metal cages that I would weld together.

Spring arrived. It rained on Wednesday and continued on Thursday and Friday. Lloyd determined that he didn't want his quail that he was due to pick up on Saturday. With having three hundred and fifty day-old quail that I had not planned on, I went into crisis mode to figure out how to take care of them. Needless to say, I was not happy. It continued to rain all week, not hard, just nasty. When it came time for Mr. Niemeyer to pick up his quail, he determined that he couldn't handle them. Suddenly I had three hundred and fifty more day-old quail. It was a full-time job changing paper, adding dry straw, adding feed, cleaning up the waters, etc. It was no longer fun. When I had an opportunity to sell my quail operation for what I had invested in it, I sold it. I didn't even take time to discuss it with my wife before making that decision.

Now, more than twenty years later, it would be nice to raise a few quail, but I sure wouldn't want to have another Georgia Quail Farm incubator, 'cause I know I would end up filling it with quail eggs. If I filled it with quail eggs, I wouldn't be having fun anymore. If I mentioned my thoughts about raising quail again to my wife, I wonder how supportive of me she would be. She has always been supportive of my wild ideas, and even supported building a house out of straw before most people had heard of the concept

Animals I Have Hated

A Twig & A Feather

While living in Payson, Arizona, my wife, Judy, and I had a garden that included, among other things, twenty-seven fruit trees. Even though we had hummingbirds in abundance, we added a feeder to attract more. We also had a cat that lived most of its time indoors, but went out several times a day.

On one occasion, she showed up at the back door muttering. Judy went to check on what she wanted. She had a small twig sticking from one side of her mouth, and a small feather from the other. Judy opened the door to see better. The cat opened her mouth and meowed. As she did so, a hummingbird flew out of her mouth. Apparently the hummer was unharmed.

After that, on a daily basis, she brought a hummingbird to Judy, and when she opened her mouth to tell Judy about it, the hummingbird would fly away unharmed.

Apparently she never learned to eat hummingbirds, but she liked to tout her expertise in catching them. We all have various abilities; sometimes we just use those abilities to show off; other times we use those abilities to make money or to help others.

Boot & Boots

Judy and I bought a one-and-a-half-acre lot south of Castroville, Texas. The lot was covered with typical South Texas scrub, including black brush, mesquite, agarita, and acacia. We decided that we would leave the lot with the maximum vegetation on it, so one could say that it was naturally xeriscaped. Some of our friends thought that zeroscaped would be a better term.

After we purchased it, we found that a neighbor took in stray dogs and allowed them the run of the neighborhood. When we started clearing a house site, we found that the neighbor's dogs thought that our property was theirs. Regularly we had to argue with them. No matter how many times we won the argument, when we would come back after being gone for a few days, they had reclaimed the property.

After the house site was cleared, we built a house and moved in. We had two cats that had to learn to live with dogs. As a result, they spent most of their time inside. One of the cats, "Boots," would periodically go out to entice the dogs to chase her. With a blood-thirsty pack in hot pursuit, she would run under very thorny shrubs.

Since we had not finished the house, we had a ladder set against the roof. Since the dogs had not learned to climb a ladder at that time, the cats were safe on the ladder. They learned that if they sat on the ladder and stared into the window, we would let them in. Were we trained, or were the cats trained?

The house we built was energy-efficient. The walls were twenty inches thick, and the windows were placed to the outside.

Opening a window was difficult for a person who was vertically challenged. Judy was so challenged.

We moved in before a screen door was installed. Months passed without the screen door being installed. Judy started leaving the front door open when it was pleasant outside, for light and ventilation. One day one of the neighbor's knee-high curs walked into the house, picked up one of my steel-toed boots, and departed. We never saw that boot again.

When I got home, Judy was indignant. By the next night, I had installed a temporary one-strand electric fence, and turned on the current at dark. Our neighbors had twenty-two free-running dogs at that time. We know, because we heard each one of them yelp as it tried to invade our property. Judy savored each yelp. Boots learned about how the electric fence affected dogs and spent a lot of time close to it trying to entice the dogs to chase her. Occasionally they were tempted beyond their power to resist, but they learned fast. Then she started moving beyond the fence to entice them. When they did, her flag would be high until she got close to the fence; it would drop as she passed under, and then be raised on the other side. Obviously she knew what she was doing, and she was having fun. I have met some people like that, and after watching Boots, I decided that when they entice me with an offer that is too good to be true, I need to resist the urge to give chase.

Time has passed. The temporary electric fence seemed to be permanent, but we have now installed a chain link fence around the property. Maybe it is time that we got a dog or three to chase Boots and steal a work boot or two.

Cassie

We were living in a small subdivision south of Castroville, Texas. One day a dirty gray kitten showed up with very matted fur and appeared to be starving. Judy fed it some milk. It did not leave, so Judy fed it again. Suddenly it seemed this might be one of those never-ending stories, with the sentence "it did not leave, so Judy fed it again" repeated over and over.

In time the cat started cleaning itself up. We discovered that rather than being a gray cat, it was a white cat with some dark-colored blotches on it. We also discovered that it was a very long-haired cat. As it put on weight, it started bullying our other cats. At the time, we figured it was about four months old. I strongly suggested to Judy that if she intended to keep that cat, or if that cat intended on living at our house, she should take it to the vet and get it fixed. She did. We learned from the vet that this cat was an adult and had already had at least one litter of kittens.

The cat continued to fill out and to take better care of herself and to become more of a bully. Soon it was our dominant cat. Six months passed, and one day Judy was down at the road with the cat. One of the neighbors stopped and exclaimed, "That's what became of Cassie." The cat would have nothing to do with our neighbor.

Over the next few weeks I learned the story of Cassie. We adopted that name, since she already had it for over a year before we ever saw her. Our neighbors had bought Cassie and a young tomcat down in Houston for a reported price of five hundred dollars apiece. They intended to breed them, sell kittens, and make money. Since the purchase of the cats had been substantial, and since they did not have a lot of extra money, they put the cats outside with the idea that they could earn their living by catching rats and mice that lived under their mobile home.

Those highfalutin cats did not know how to catch rats and mice. In time, Cassie had two litters of kittens. The family had expected the highfalutin male to mate with the highfalutin female. That did not happen. Alley tomcats showed up and mated with Cassie. None of Cassie's offspring resembled her. None of them had any value. Therefore it became even more important that Cassie learn to go out and catch rats and mice so she could be a contributing member of that family. And that is how Cassie, in a near-starved condition, ended up at our house.

To this day Cassie will have nothing to do with our neighbors. They ask about her. When I pick up Cassie and carry her towards their property, Cassie's claws come out, and I am reminded of my sister's vicious cat, Fluffy.

My mother had Weimar fixed, and I had Cassie fixed. I wonder if the trait of fixing highfalutin animals that belong to other people is genetic.

Montezuma's Quail

J udy and I, with our friends Rose Ann and James, traveled to the Davis Mountains. Judy and Rose Ann had been roommates, and we had married about three weeks apart some years before. We went to the Davis Mountains State Park and stayed at the Indian Lodge to celebrate our joint anniversaries.

We hoped to see the Fools or Mears Quail, which is now called the Montezuma's Quail. We missed them Thursday evening. Friday morning and Friday evening were not any better. Saturday morning one of our group saw two of the quail. By Saturday evening most of the group was worried about not seeing them at all. Sunday morning we checked one feeder, and there were none. As we headed to the second feeder, a park volunteer drove up and told us that Montezuma's Quail were feeding at the second feeder. He said that to see them we had to be quiet and approach cautiously.

We drove to the second feeder and parked on the far side of the parking lot. We quietly got out of the car and quietly closed the doors. As we quietly walked up to the blind, another park volunteer roared up in his loud pickup. He parked as close to the blind as he could and got out of the pickup and slammed the door. He called to us in a loud voice, **"You got to be quiet, or you will scare them."** He then strode up to the blind wall while we were continuing to walk quietly. After looking through the porthole, he announced in a voice that could be heard at one hundred feet, **"One of them is gone now, but if you keep quiet, the other will come back."** He then strode off, got in his pickup, slammed the door, started the pickup, and roared off.

YOU GOTTA BE QUIET!!

We walked up to the blind wall. There were no quail in sight. Two Montezuma Quail did come out of hiding as the ranger had said they would. If a person hates his job as much as that volunteer hated his job, I wonder, why does he volunteer? Maybe he loves his job, but has no clue how to get along with wildlife or with people. In that case, maybe he should be volunteering to work at a slaughterhouse. That park volunteer taught me that volunteers need as much supervision as paid employees, and maybe more. He also taught me that if there is any way to avoid it, I should not do things that seriously interfere with others finding joy. Should I suggest this to my friends in law enforcement?

Montezuma's Quail

To A Mockingbird

My family gathered at a South Texas graveyard to bury Papa. He had lived most of his life in South Texas, and he was being buried there. Beside the tent that covered the grave was an Arizona Ash tree. It was all of twelve feet high. Pastor Biar led the service.

As the service started, I remembered my first memories of Papa. Back in the nineteen forties on a moonlit night, he had been irrigating a cotton field, and I heard him singing "Amapola" in his clear tenor voice. He might have been a quarter of a mile away, but his voice carried through the clear night air. I remembered him singing the same song when hoeing cotton. A cousin told me that his first memories of Papa were when he would sing "Amapola" while swinging a grubbing hoe. A few years later, I heard a recording of Enrico Caruso singing "Amapola," and my first thought was, "How did Caruso learn Papa's song?" Don't get me wrong, this was not the only song he sang, but it was the first one that I remember.

As Pastor Biar continued with the service, a mockingbird started singing in the tree beside the funeral tent. It brought memories flooding back. As the forties drifted into the fifties, I remember Papa singing about waking up on Mockingbird Hill. For several years, whenever we were out and he would hear a mockingbird, he would break into that song.

We then sang the first verse of "Amazing Grace." We had planned to sing it a cappella, but the mockingbird joined in. By the second verse, a second mockingbird had joined the orchestra. We continued through "Amazing Grace" with the mockingbird duet.

As the service continued with the scripture readings, the mockingbirds appeared to be trying to drown Pastor Biar out. Cousin Fred, who is the son of one pastor and the brother of another pastor, quietly walked over to the tree and attempted to shoo the mockingbirds away. I silently rooted for the mockingbirds, and as I found out later, several other members of the family were rooting for the mockingbirds. They would not cooperate, so Cousin Fred shook the tree. The mockingbirds left, but before Cousin Fred was three steps away from the tree, they were back, singing their hearts out.

Lord, thank You for mockingbirds.

We finished the service with the mockingbirds and Pastor Biar competing for the attention of the mourners, and I was thinking about Papa's love for birds.

I do not know what Pastor Biar thought of his competition, but all I can say is, "Lord, thank You for mockingbirds." To this day, whenever I hear a mockingbird, I think of that service.

Animals I Have Hated

Rosie

My sister, Mary, adopted Rosie from the pound in July, 2005. She decided Rosie must be part Basenji, because she does not bark and she has the Basenji look to her. Shortly after the adoption, Rosie was diagnosed with distemper, but after Mary paid some expensive vet bills, Rosie recovered.

When she had been in the backyard and wanted to come into the house, she learned to ring a bell. Rosie did not like to go out in the front yard. She would meet us at the front door; and in welcoming us, she might step outside, but immediately she went back into the house. Rosie is a loveable and rambunctious dog who, and I am using "who" rather than "which," because in many ways she seems human, has a very long tongue. On more than one occasion, I knew that I was safe from that tongue washing my face, but found that I was mistaken.

Daisy, Momma's rat terrier, and Momma grew old together. Daisy protected Momma and would growl and fiercely attack anyone who came near Momma without Daisy's permission. She would even attack the Pastor. We talked about which one would die first, Daisy or Momma, not the Pastor, and how the other would react when that happened. We knew that it would be hard on the survivor. Daisy died first.

Mary brought Rosie over to visit on several occasions, and Rosie would curl up on Momma's feet as Momma was sitting in her favorite chair. On July 3, 2006, when Mary went home, Rosie decided that she was already at home. She barely raised her head to bid Mary "good night." During all of the time she lived with Momma, her favorite place was curled up on Momma's feet as

Momma sat in her chair. When Momma ate, Rosie did not beg. When the rest of us ate, Rosie begged. When Momma went to bed, Rosie curled up beside the bed. There was a bond between the old lady and the relatively-young dog.

Rosie on duty.

As Momma got frailer and frailer, we discussed how we could keep from having to move her into a nursing home. She equated a nursing home with prison, and prison was not an option. Mary and Wayne moved in with Momma, so they could help Rosie take care of her, but they had to work during the day. Our friend Linda came and stayed with her most days. When Linda's health would not let her continue, there were private duty nurses. They were expensive. There just were not any good options, not even expensive ones.

No matter who was with Momma, Rosie was on duty. When Momma would start to get up during the night, Rosie would rush in to Mary and wake Mary up. If Mary was a little slow in getting up to help Momma, that long tongue would come out and wash Mary's face until she was awake and moving to help Momma.

During the day, if the caregiver was not in the room with Momma when she needed something, Rosie would fetch the caregiver. As Momma got even weaker, Rosie would go get Mary when Momma would wake up, even before Momma started to think about getting up. Obviously, they had a method of communication.

In January, 2008, a decision was made by Momma's medical staff that she would not make it to Easter, so she was placed on In-Home Hospice Care. Momma could be stubborn. When she found that she was on Hospice Care, and she knew that the medical staff expected her to die, that stubbornness kicked in, and she resisted following her doctors' prognosis. She lived to celebrate Easter. Then she lived to celebrate Easter again.

Meanwhile, Rosie remained at her side helping her, except for a little run in the backyard each day when she knew there was someone to look after Momma.

Rosie

Epilogue

By August, 2009, eighteen months after she was placed on Hospice Care, it became evident that Momma could not last over another day or two. My daughter Dana, her husband JT, and their three daughters drove down from Minot, North Dakota, hoping to at least make it in time for the funeral. By the time they arrived, Momma was comatose most of the time. Often she would not wake up when she was turned to prevent bed sores, or when her sheets were changed.

As soon as Dana arrived, we told her of Momma's condition, and she quietly walked into Momma's room carrying 7-week-old Fornie. Momma's eyes popped open, and she said, "What a beautiful baby. May I hold her?" She had not spoken that much in a week. Dana put Fornie in Momma's arms. Momma held Fornie for about fifteen minutes and talked to Dana and Fornie. Momma was worn out, so Dana took Fornie, and Momma went back to sleep. On three different occasions over the next several days, when Dana walked quietly into Momma's room with Fornie, Momma woke up and asked to hold Fornie. Somehow or other, Momma knew when Fornie came into the room.

JT's leave from the Air Force was about to expire, so the family loaded up and headed home. About the time they got to Dallas, Momma died. She had lived long enough to get acquainted with another great-granddaughter.

We buried Momma beside Papa. That oak tree where the mockingbirds sang, had grown. One mockingbird joined us, but it did not sing. Rosie, now a rambunctious middle-aged dog, continues to take care of her family.

Animals I Have Hated

About Nordmeyer, LLC

Nordmeyer, LLC
Castroville, TX 78009-2120

Nordmeyer, LLC, is owned by the Nordmeyer family and was set up for:

- Their consulting business (stucco, mortar, pozzolans, green building, and building façade forensics),
- Their kayak guiding service (www.TxNatureKayaking.com), and
- Their writing and publishing business (www.NordyBooks.com).

For obvious reasons, the writing and publishing portion of the business is commonly referred to as Nordy Books. "Nordy Books" was set up to publish and market books that are written in whole or in part by Herb Nordmeyer. Those books fall into the following categories:

Cancer,

Construction-related,

Devotions,

Kayak-related, and

Stories with life lessons.

Go to www.nordybooks.com for an update on which books are currently available and which ones will be published in the near future.

Other Books & Booklets by Herb Nordmeyer

We Heard The Wings of Angels–thirty-two devotions by & for cancer patients and their families
Edited by Judy and Herb Nordmeyer
Published 1999

Cancer–An Intense House Guest–A practical guide for living with cancer
By Judy and Herb Nordmeyer
Published 2008

The Stucco Book–The Basics–The first of three informative guides to stuccoing written in a humorous style
By Herb Nordmeyer
Published 2012

Go to www.nordybooks.com to find out where to obtain these and other books and booklets by Herb Nordmeyer.

About Herb Nordmeyer

Herb Nordmeyer is a leading stucco authority and has been published regularly in trade journals and ASTM publications. As a result, he is in demand as a speaker, an educator, an on-site consultant to solve construction issues, and an expert witness. Besides being admired for his knowledge, integrity, and candor, he is also known for a dry wit that is honed as sharply as is his mastery of the stucco industry.

When not helping people with stucco problems, Herb is a prolific writer. Besides writing religious devotional pieces, he has developed several booklets that help cancer patients deal with spiritual issues, and stories with life lessons. He is an experienced wilderness kayaking guide and instructor. Herb lives in Castroville, Texas, with his wife, Judy, and the occasional stray cat or guinea fowl.

This is Herb's first full-length book of stories with life lessons, but two more are in the works. Over the next several years we expect to see them and also more books related to construction. His kayaking clients are insisting that he write a book on recreational kayaking.

CPSIA information can be obtained at www.ICGtesting.com
Printed in the USA
LVOW101408290212

270955LV00004B/1/P